YOLO COUNTY LIBRARY
YOLO COUNTY LIBRARY
226 BUCKEYE STREET
WOODLAND, CA 95695-2600

DISCARDED

IDEAS FOR GREAT
HOME OFFICES

By the Editors of Sunset Books

D0470701

ARCHITECT: SANBORN DESIGNS INCORPORATED

747.79
IDE

A bedroom armoire is geared up for office action (see page 63).

Sunset Publishing Corporation ■ Menlo Park, California

Shelves for books and magazines needn't be boring; for additional ideas, see pages 104–107.

By Digital Demand

What a change a few years can bring—especially when the subject is working from home. When Sunset published the book *Home Offices & Workspaces* in the mid-'80s, there were no notebook computers, fax machines, or cellular flip phones—now standard tools for many home-based workers. The numbers of telecommuters and small-business owners were beginning to rise; now they've soared to more than 40 million and are still climbing.

With this all-new title, Sunset brings the home office into the mid-'90s, and we've wrapped it in the colorful style you've come to expect from our popular "Ideas for Great" format. You'll find a kaleidoscope of office designs, products, and creative solutions on the following pages.

Many people assisted us in gathering the material for this book. We'd especially like to thank Brian Brand, Daniel Gregory, Donald Hensman, Van-Martin Rowe, and Beverly McGuire. Also, our thanks go to Eurodesign Ltd.; Just Chairs; Herman Miller, Inc.; Moss Lighting; Navigator Systems; Smart Interiors, Inc.; and Techline Studios.

Cover: This inviting home office combines elegance, efficiency, and a playful sense of history. The bird's-eye maple cabinetry borrows details from Biedermeier furniture, which became popular in Europe in the early 1800s. Interior design: Karen Adelson Interiors. Cover design by Vasken Guiragossian. Photography by Michael Bruk.

SUNSET BOOKS

VP, Sales & Marketing
Richard A. Smeby

VP, Editorial Director
Bob Doyle

Production Director
Lory Day

Art Director
Vasken Guiragossian

Book Editor
Scott Atkinson

Coordinating Editor
Linda J. Selden

Copy Editor
Marcia Williamson

Design
Joe di Chiarro

Illustrations
Bill Oetinger

Principal Photographer
Philip Harvey

Photo Director
JoAnn Masaoka Van Atta

4 5 6 7 8 9 0 QPD/QPD 9 8 7 6 5 4 3 2 1 0

Copyright © 1995 Sunset Publishing Corporation, Menlo Park, CA 94025. First edition. All rights reserved, including the right of reproduction in whole or in part in any form.
ISBN 0-376-01755-4
Library of Congress Catalog Card Number: 94-069957
Printed in the United States.
Visit our website at
www.sunsetbooks.com

CONTENTS

Getting Down to Business

Each week, more than 40 million people grab a coffee mug and pad across a room, down a hall, or upstairs into home offices. Some are part-time telecommuters linked to headquarters via telephones, personal computers, and/or overnight mail. Others are full-time employees working from home. A growing number are small-business owners setting forth on their own.

These workers are taking advantage of new technology and a growing acceptance of home-based business. But you don't need to be a "professional" to appreciate having a quiet, organized work space at home. Many homeowners need a place to track personal finances and correspondence or just a well-set-up spot for working with the family's multimedia computer.

Whatever your home-office needs, this book can supply the inspiration, design ideas, and practical data you'll need to plan an efficient and comfortable work space.

Why the Move Home?

Experts cite three converging reasons for the dramatic rise in home-based business: advances in personal computers and other office electronics, corporate downsizing, and dissatisfaction with urban stress and long, tiresome commutes.

The computer can arm a home-based worker with much the same

Plain-paper fax

power and polish as the big players. And new telecommunications technology makes it possible to access information and transfer finished work almost instantly.

Many established businesses are taking a look at telecommuting as a way to motivate workers, solve overcrowding, ride out economic changes, and grapple with tough new commuting laws. Telecommuting is also growing because the nature of much work is changing—away from producing goods and toward information services.

The appeal of home-based work goes beyond the opportunity to make your morning conference calls in sweatshirt and jeans or a bathrobe. Many home workers cite newly found (noncommute) time, lower stress, and lower overhead as major benefits. Others experience a better balance between work and family life. Many two-earner families resolve conflicting business and home duties when one (or both) adult works at home.

Empowering Products

Try asking, "Do I really need to be in an office setting to do my work, or to communicate with colleagues, or to send and receive information?" If the answer is no, a light bulb may go off in your head. With today's communications technology, it may not matter if you're working in the financial district or in Timbuktu.

As the personal computer keeps gaining in power and performance, it continues to shrink in both size and cost. Fax machines, modems, answering machines or voice-mail services, and laser printers can all help a small business look and sound big. Notebook computers, cellular phones, pagers, portable faxes, and built-in modems can let you take the home office on the road—from breakfast nook to deck to car as the day progresses.

Working from home will only get easier. Electronic mail, online services, and the Internet are just a few of the digital conveniences that are daily changing the face of how we acquire and transmit information.

Are You Comfortable?

Another boon in office awareness is that it's now OK to admit you're uncomfortable—and then do something about it. Take, for example, the development of form-fitting, adjustable chairs and workstations. Many of us were instructed to sit up pine-tree-straight—first in school, then later in the corporate environment. The assumption was that if you were too comfortable, you were relaxing—and not doing your work.

Fortunately, that's all changing. Ergonomic experts and manufactur-

A graphic artist's desktop computer is placed for working efficiency—and to take advantage of a great view.

Cellular flip phone

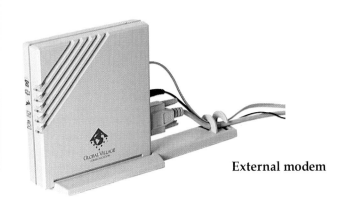

External modem

ers are reshaping how we view our attitudes toward both the work environment and personal health. You'll discover a range of ergonomic products and guidelines in this book.

Riding the Design Wave

When the home office surge began, options in furniture and other equipment were limited. What was available was designed for offices, not homes. The personal computer was so new we didn't really know what to do with it.

But now homeowners, designers, and manufacturers are taking a figurative step back, and a second wave of office design is the result. After all, if it's your home, why dress it like a steno pool?

Attractive, home-scaled furnishings, space-saving products and hardware, more refined textures, and both bolder and subtler colors are aimed at complementing, not clashing with, your home design. Even electronics makers are beginning to rethink their previously predictable beiges and grays.

But Is It Right for You?

Still, working at home is not for everyone. Some people report a struggle with loneliness, at least initially. Some feel out of the loop; others miss the "water-cooler" chats. Discipline can be a problem. Almost everyone reports that working at home requires some adjustment.

One key, experts say, is to maintain contact with peers and suppliers. Start a support group; plan networking lunches with colleagues. Part-time telecommuting might be a good way to test the waters (see pages 122–123).

Check the Fine Print

If you plan to operate a home business, you'll need to know the local zoning ordinances that govern your options. In some areas, the use of

detached buildings, separate office entrances, and even signs is prohibited. Some counties and municipalities also limit the amount of a home's square footage that can be devoted to a business. In other areas, you cannot store goods in your home or make retail transactions there.

You may also need to get a local business license and pay local business fees. And of course, there may be taxes, insurance, and employee benefits to consider.

It pays to get sound business advice. This is not a book about small business or finance, but much good information is already available elsewhere; see pages 126–127 for starters.

Ready to Begin?

You've thought it through. What's the next step? Perhaps it's time to find the place to hang your shingle. That's where this book comes in.

It leads off with "A Planning Primer," a simple sequential course in office design. Basic points include location, layout, and style options. We also offer both ergonomic and organizational guidelines.

Then come two big color photo galleries. The first highlights self-contained rooms. The second features found-space or shared-space alternatives. Some of the offices pictured in these pages are quite grand, and some are as small as the space beneath your stairs.

The final chapter, "A Shopper's Guide," is a guidebook to the rapidly changing world of workstations, computers, and communications and the baffling lingo these subjects have spawned. You'll also find an introduction to the expanding world of online services. The chapter ends with a resource list for further access and information.

Are you ready to get down to business? If so, simply turn the page.

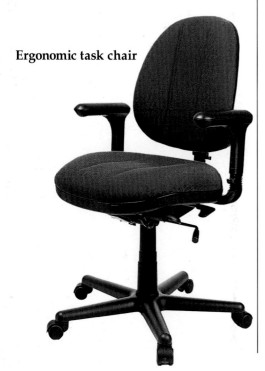

Ergonomic task chair

A self-contained, wood-trimmed office is screened by double doors, yet maintains a link with both house and garden via interior and exterior glazing.

ARCHITECT: JIM OLSON AND MATTHEW STANNARD/OLSON SUNDBERG ARCHITECTS

INTERIOR DESIGNER: BAUER INTERIOR DESIGN

A PLANNING PRIMER

Bringing your work space home is an exciting idea. But it raises some practical questions. Where will you find the room for a home office? What, really, do you need in the way of equipment and furniture? What's the best way to set things up, taking into account your personal work style as well as the nature of your work?

This chapter helps you structure your thoughts about planning an effective work environment. The photo galleries of successful home offices and workstations (pages 31–89) provide plenty of design inspiration. Pages 112–127 give detailed information on the electronics and telecommunications that can instantly link home-based workers to a wider world.

While grappling with the intricacies of computers and fax modems, don't forget the touches that can make your new space a comfortable, attractive part of your home.

A 10- by 12-foot guest room was the backdrop for this colorful, efficient office, sealed from household noise by glazed interior doors. Colorful laminate countertops save space, create inviting angles, and allow the resident attorney to roll from task to task.

TAKING STOCK

Unless you live in a mansion where parlors and studies abound, finding room for a home office may seem quite a challenge. Actually, though, potential office space is almost always lurking in plain view. Identifying it simply requires a shift of perspective, which this section can help you achieve.

Perhaps you're fortunate enough to have a spare room. But the most common way to squeeze in a home office is to borrow space from an existing room—diplomatically, so as not to disturb the room's original purpose. Or perhaps you'd like to be able to spread out more, taking over an unused attic, basement, or garage. Of course, a truly luxurious answer might be an office addition, achieved either by extending your house up or out or by building a structure elsewhere on your property.

Think ahead. Where might your family be in five years? Will a spare bedroom open up as kids depart for college? Could a second-story addition house both your home office and the master suite you've been dreaming of? Could a detached cottage-office later become an in-law unit?

WHERE WILL IT GO?

Up, down, and around: the search is on, and people are discovering office space in the far reaches of their homes. Still, some options are better than others. Here's a look at the possibilities.

Spare bedroom. If you have an unused bedroom, it can make an ideal office space. You can tailor it specifically for your business—and at the end of the workday, you just close the door and walk away. (And remember, claiming a tax deduction is most straightforward when you have a room used exclusively for business.)

Guest bedroom. A rung down in convenience from a spare bedroom, a guest room or media room may nonetheless yield adequate space for work. But beware: TV wars and other squabbles can intrude if the area is used by several family members. And what if a guest comes to stay while you're on a tough deadline?

Still, if you're cramped for space, a guest room is a reasonable option. The key is to make the room flexible. Choose office furnishings that can be closed up or moved aside during non-office hours. This needn't mean expensive custom pieces: an interior designer found a fold-away table from a camping store just fine for laying out samples; it stores along one side of the closet when not in use.

Master bedroom. Most designers agree that having an office in your bedroom is a bad idea. Picture arising in the morning to the clutter from yesterday's business headache. And the light and noise from a late-night accounting session won't do much for your mate's disposition.

But if the privacy and convenience of a bedroom office are strong attractions, there are ways to minimize the negatives. A decorative screen, knee wall, bookcase, or other divider can block both noise and light. Shoji panels, glass pocket doors, and other movable dividers are also options. And with a modular wall unit or rolltop desk, you can get your work out of sight when it's time to relax.

Living/family room. Again, this spot has a strike or two against it. Unless you're highly organized, you may feel that work is taking over your house. And unless you live alone, you won't have much privacy.

Use modular cabinetry, a room divider, a change of level, or a decorative screen to help define—and contain—the office area.

If you have high ceilings or could raise the present ceiling, you might consider designing a loft adjacent to living quarters. Loft dwellers report an agreeable mix of access and privacy, and the space below the loft can serve other purposes.

Interior Options

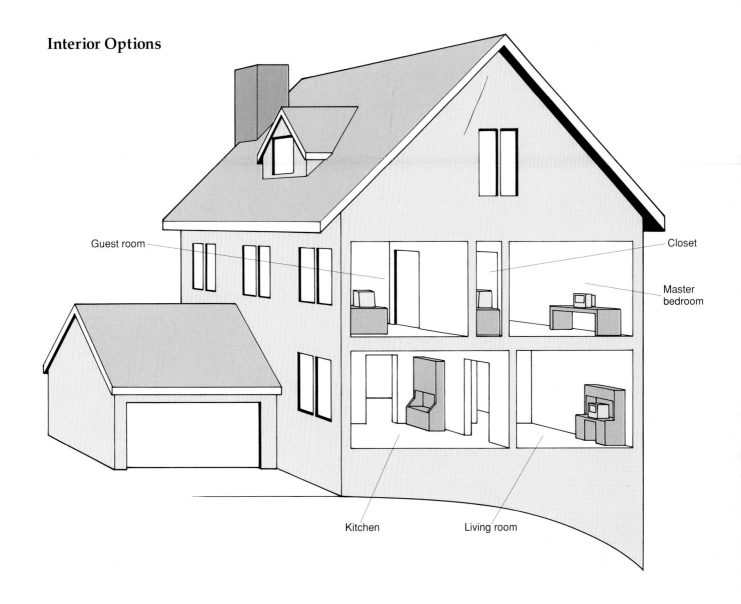

Guest room · Closet · Master bedroom · Kitchen · Living room

Dining room. This can be a candidate, especially if you rarely dine there. One plus: a large dining-room table allows the visually oriented plenty of space to spread out papers and files.

Order, order, order is the key to a dining-room office. You really need to be able to close off your work space during meals—to protect your papers as well as your digestion.

Kitchen. Can a kitchen make a decent work space? It depends on the nature of your work, on your need for privacy, and on how boisterous your family is. Some home workers like the sense of connection to the pulse of a busy household; others feel constantly distracted and exposed to interruption. There's also more potential for damage to papers and other business materials. But if the site still appeals to you, consider whether you might incorporate your work space into a breakfast area or build it into a cabinet run.

Closet. If your space needs are modest, don't overlook the opportunity presented by a spare closet (if there is such a thing). A 20-inch-deep space is the bare-bones minimum, but even this depth can house a built-in counter with storage units below and shelves above. With bifold or hinged doors, you can seal off the space when it's not in use (and if you're storing electronic equipment, louvered doors would provide ventilation).

Be on the lookout for other "found" space. How about the niche under the stairs? Or the utility room? Could an existing closet in an adjacent room be colonized as part of an office next door?

Porch or sunroom. You can also convert a porch or sunroom to office space, though you'll probably need to build up the floor and walls, insulate, ventilate, and add temperature controls. What about pouring a small slab for a prefabricated greenhouse addition?

Pop-out. Maybe all your office plans need is a slight "push"—like the one furnished by a 24-inch wall extension or a bay window unit. Cantilevered pop-outs can bypass some building restrictions because they don't need additional foundations.

Attic conversion. There's lots of potential here if you have the headroom: by code, it must be at least 7 feet over half the floor area. Side walls may be too low for standing, but not for sitting. Try stretching countertops along these areas. Skylights and dormers add headroom and bring in light and air.

Attic floor joists may not be intended for "live" weight; if necessary, beef them up. Are there wires and pipes? You'll need to reroute them.

Basement conversion. Dank and dungeon-like, our image of the typical unfinished basement is less than compelling. But if you can get past the creepy-movie associations, you may have found a large private space for your office. Split-level homes are prime candidates, as one or more walls may open out to light and an access door.

Moisture-proofing is crucial. Masonry walls should be sealed, insulated, then covered with gypsum wallboard or paneling. Build up the floor

Remodeling Options

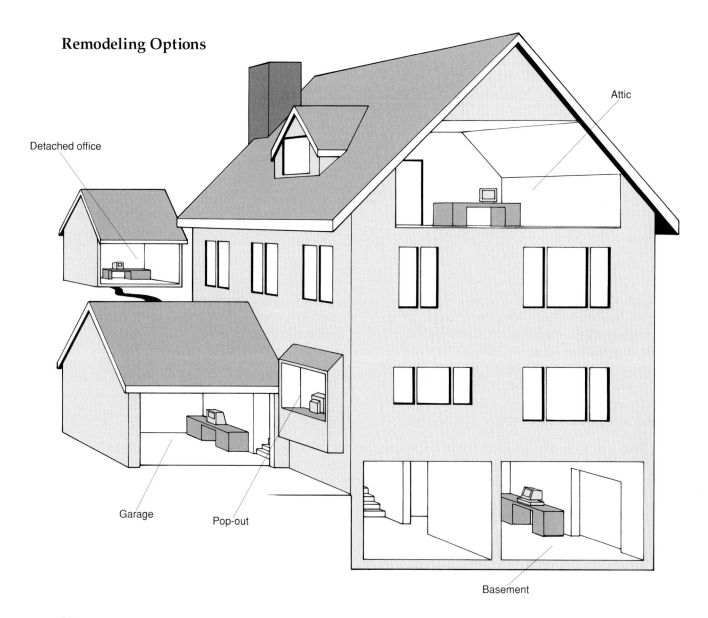

Detached office

Attic

Garage

Pop-out

Basement

in the same way. If you can't get rid of heating ducts and plumbing pipes, paint them jazzy colors or simply box them in with more wallboard.

Garage conversion. With a little insulation, a weathertight door, a skylight, and a built-up floor, a garage—especially one that's detached from the house—could make a great home office. You could even add French doors and a sunny pocket deck.

Logistically, though, a garage remodel may prove daunting. Routing wires, pipes (if necessary), and heating ducts can be expensive. And where will the car go? In some communities, you'll have to add a new garage or carport to make up for the off-street parking space you've lost.

Adding on. When it's remodeling time, you can go up, down, or sideways—add a second story or basement, build on a one- or two-story addition, or extend the front, back, or side of the house.

Adding laterally may be the best way to expand your house when you have a big enough lot—especially if you will have clients or employees using the office.

But if your house already fills your lot, if you want to preserve garden space, or if you yearn for views that lie beyond your neighbor's rooftop, going up might be the answer. Could you combine an office with a new second-story master suite?

A detached office. For some, there's nothing like grabbing a mug of coffee and a snack, then "commuting" to a secluded backyard office or pool-house studio. Perhaps a little-used guest house or revamped potting shed could become the place to hang your shingle. Or you could start from scratch, and get it right the first time.

But while a new building is the ultimate office solution, it could prove an especially expensive option. Besides the labor of building a separate foundation, walls, and roof, you'll have to extend utilities to the site. You'll probably wish (and may be required) to include a bathroom, which means routing both supply and waste pipes. You'll need an independent heat source. If this is your first experience working at home, you might want to try it out on a smaller scale first.

The "floating" office. Finally, remember that there's no rule that says your office must be confined to one room. If you're cramped for space, why not split things up? For example, try relegating

EVALUATING YOUR SPACE

Before you rush off to empty the linen closet or dry out the basement, work out a wish list for the kind of office you're looking for. Some of your requirements will be structural or equipment-based; others will relate more to your own personal work style. As plans take shape, test them against the questions listed below (each of these is explored more fully later on).

■ Are the area's heating, cooling, and ventilation systems adequate to handle your office needs?

■ Will you have to add electrical circuits or extend phone lines?

■ Is the lighting—both natural and artificial—sufficient? Are there problems with glare? Do you need a view, or would one cause needless distraction?

■ What about privacy? Will you be disturbed by family members? Will household noise be transmitted over the phone? Will you be able to concentrate with loud traffic or neighbors outside?

■ Do you need a separate area for a postal scale, copier, project bins, or sample books?

■ Do you need extra bookshelves or space to display products?

■ If clients call on you, will the space project a suitable image? Is there room for a conference table and seating? When visitors approach your office, will your entire house (and family) be on display?

■ Do you need a separate outside entrance?

tasks like writing and telephoning to one quiet spot while equipping a less private area elsewhere with files, fax, and copier.

Not everyone needs a formal office. We've talked to numerous people who prefer to go mobile, toting a laptop computer and portable phone from bedroom to dining room to deck as the day progresses. By adding a cellular phone, voice-mail service, and a built-in fax modem, these floating offices can also move part-time to a moving car—or even to the beach.

A Sample Base Map

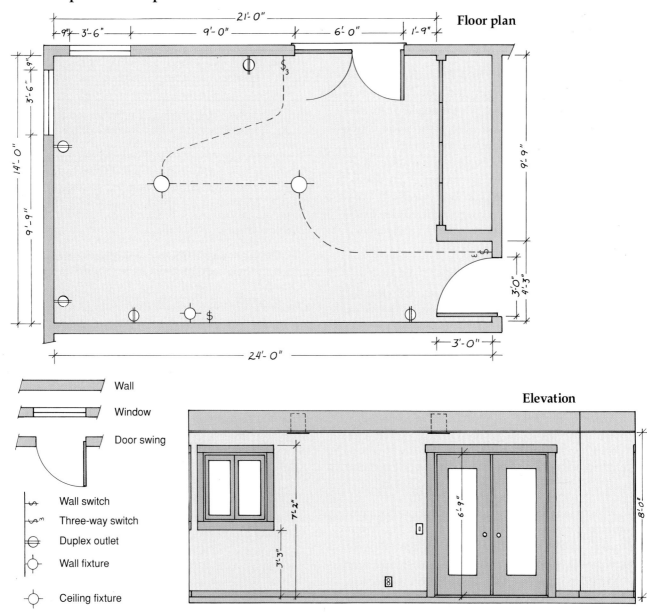

Floor plan

Wall

Window

Door swing

S Wall switch

S_3 Three-way switch

Duplex outlet

Wall fixture

Ceiling fixture

Elevation

MAKE A FLOOR PLAN

Once you've narrowed the possibilities, it helps to make a floor plan (a bird's-eye view) and one or more elevations (straight-on views) of any office area you're considering. Clear, accurate drawings help you see both problems and solutions. They also help you communicate with design professionals and showroom personnel.

Measuring the space. To begin your office survey, you'll need either a folding wooden rule or a steel measuring tape. First, sketch out your present perimeter (don't worry about scale), doodling in windows, doors, closets, and other features.

Then measure along each wall, including the sizes and locations of any openings or irregularities. Start your measurements at one corner, measuring from the corner to the first window frame or door. From this point, measure to the opposite edge of the opening and then from the opposite edge of the frame to the far corner.

Once you've noted down the increments, take an overall measurement from corner to corner. Do the measurements of the opposite walls agree? If not, something's out of whack; find out what it is.

Make any intermediate measurements needed to place a heating vent, closet, or any other feature of the wall. Note the locations of all electrical outlets, switches, and telephone jacks.

All of these measurements can be transferred directly onto a rough sketch of each elevation. In addition, you'll need to measure and record window and door heights, as well as the height of the ceiling. Be sure to note any ceiling slope or other unusual wall configuration.

Drawing a floor plan. An accurate floor plan provides a background against which you can visualize, measure, and plot the best office layout.

To draw a room to scale, most designers use ½-inch scale (¼₄ actual size). Some good drafting paper with ½-inch squares and a T-square and triangle greatly simplify matters. These and other helpful drawing tools are discussed at right.

The paper's squares will represent units of measurement. Follow the rough sketch you've made. If one wall, for example, measured 12 feet, 3 inches long, you would mark off 12¼ squares of graph paper for the length of that wall.

The sample floor plan shown on the facing page includes electrical symbols—outlets, switches, and fixtures. Be sure to include door swings, windows and skylights, and any heating ducts or returns. It's also helpful to note the direction of floor and ceiling joists, mark any bearing walls, and sketch in other features that might affect your remodeling plans. If you're considering "borrowing" space from an adjacent room or hallway, add that area to your map as well.

Making elevations. The purpose of an accurate elevation is to allow you to plan the arrangement of cabinets, equipment, and other additions against each wall in relation to features such as windows, doors, electrical outlets, and vents.

Using your rough elevation sketch (or sketches) with all dimensions measured and double-checked, draw the perimeter of each wall onto graph paper. Next, fill in all fixed features, such as windows, light fixtures, telephone jacks, and electrical outlets. Make sure you use the same scale you used for the floor plan.

Make several photocopies of each drawing. Then gather up your wish list, plus any clippings and catalogs you've collected, and get ready to start brainstorming.

TOOLS OF THE TRADE

To draw your base map (and, later, any final plans), you'll need graph paper (½-inch scale, unless the size of your space requires ¼-inch scale), an art gum eraser, a straightedge, several pencils, and a pad of tracing paper. Optional are a drafting board, a T-square, one or more triangles, a compass, a circle template, and an architect's scale. For taking room measurements, choose either a steel measuring tape or a folding wooden rule.

You can draw your base map directly on graph paper or on tracing paper placed over graph paper or a grid. Use the straightedge or T-square to draw horizontal lines. For vertical lines at a perfect right angle (such as a corner of the room), use a triangle with one edge placed over the horizontal line. To account for the space taken up by a door, set a compass to the scaled-down door's width and use it to draw the door's direction of swing.

If you have a personal computer, don't overlook the growing collection of drawing and space-planning software. Unlike earlier CAD programs aimed at professionals, these new offerings are designed for the skill levels and budgets of do-it-yourselfers.

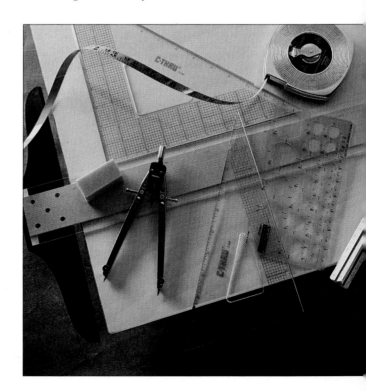

Gearing Up

Some experts have said there are only two essentials for a functional home office: a comfortable chair and a door that closes. In this age of information, we'd probably add a few items.

Whatever your leanings, it's time to block out the basics. Scan the photos and text throughout this book for ideas. Shop around, floor plan and measuring tape in hand. Talk to retailers. Look at magazines and advertisements and check out mail-order catalogs (for some leads, see pages 126–127). Dream a bit.

Then start putting your ideas on paper. Most office owners want space for desk work or paperwork, keyboard operation, telephone/fax use, and storage. A fifth space, the seating/conference area, is important to some, unnecessary to others.

In addition, consider the things that affect your overall well-being. Some of these are tangible, such as good lighting, safe wiring, and ergonomically correct design. Others, though less visible—such as the need for quiet or privacy—are no less important. Independence can be important, too; providing an under-counter refrigerator and a coffee maker or small microwave could help cut down on those distracting forays to the kitchen.

One way to save time—and your back—when planning is to use paper cutouts. Draw the outlines of any large equipment and furnishings you're considering to the same scale as your floor plan, then make several photocopies of both and cut them out. Slide the cutouts around on a copy of your map until you see a promising layout, then trace

Five Basic Layouts

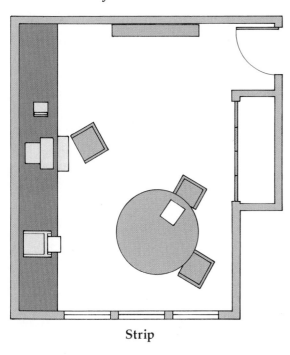

Strip

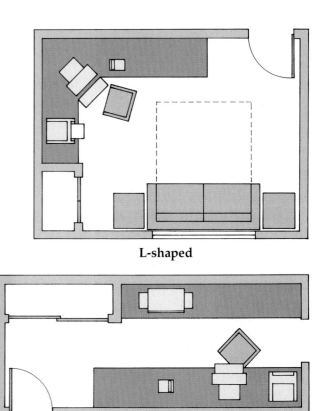

L-shaped

Corridor

the outlines onto the plan. Create and compare several layouts. Review your priorities. Then choose the setup that offers the best solution to your own individual needs.

START WITH THE DESK

Begin by blocking out major work surfaces. You might opt for a conventional desk, computer workstation, modular wall system, or built-in countertops—or any combination of these. While the traditional executive's desk promotes authority, specialized computer furnishings may offer greater efficiency. Built-in countertops lend clean design lines and save space. For a closer look at some choices, see pages 92–97.

Decide which direction you want to face as you sit at work. If you crave privacy, you may prefer to have your back to the door. You might have a hankering to locate your desk so you can look out a window. If you plan to meet with others in your space, the traditional outward-facing desk arrangement may be best.

Several basic space configurations are shown below. The *strip* layout is limiting and requires more steps, but it tucks into the smallest space. The *L-shaped* layout makes use of often-awkward corner areas and helps you combine a computer station with a standard desk or countertop. The *corridor* or *parallel* layout is an executive's standby: many companies sell coordinated credenzas and shelf units to back up the traditional desk. If you have the space for it, the *U-shaped* layout is considered the most functional, requiring the fewest steps to access everything. Your layout needn't follow the room's walls. What about an angled configuration?

Whether work surfaces are unfitted or built in, they should be at least 20 inches deep. If you type or use a computer regularly, you'll need at least 18 inches of clear space on one or both sides of the machine for materials. Large monitors require a lot of counter depth; could you angle one into an otherwise wasted corner?

Many people don't realize that computer work surfaces need to be lower than desk height. (For guidelines, see "A Look at Ergonomics" on pages 18–19.) Mounting a pullout keyboard shelf or tray below the desk top may solve the problem; an adjustable chair can fine-tune the workstation to your own dimensions.

(Continued on page 20)

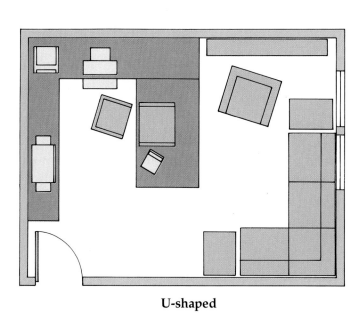

U-shaped

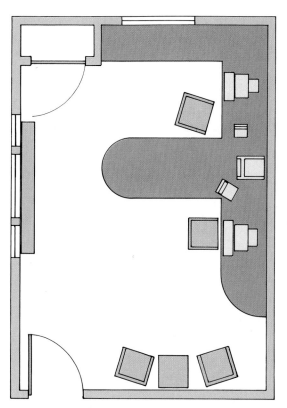

Double-L with shared peninsula

A LOOK AT ERGONOMICS

The term *ergonomics* refers to human engineering—that is, designing equipment, furniture, and work spaces to be both efficient and comfortable for human use.

Until recently, little attention was paid to such concerns. But as computer use increased, workers spending long hours at terminals began to show signs of physical strain that had not before been associated with desk work. Frequent complaints of backaches, headaches, neck and shoulder tension, wrist and hand injuries, eyestrain, and general irritability led to the emergence of the ergonomics design field.

The findings of ergonomists, some of which are discussed below and illustrated on the facing page, are a helpful guide in furnishing a home office.

The desk. As a general starting point, the surface used for writing and other paperwork should be about 28½ inches from the floor. However, for comfortable work at a keyboard, the surface should stand lower—about 24 to 27 inches high.

But more important than absolute heights are the body angles and stresses that are induced by the interrelated heights of keyboard, computer monitor, and chair.

The keyboard. You should be able to type with both arms relaxed at your sides, forearms at right angles to your body, and wrists in a neutral position. Keyboard angle should be neutral (as shown) or, according to some studies, at a slightly negative angle.

An articulating keyboard tray (AKT) can be positioned at any height and at any distance from the desk edge or computer screen; use this or a simpler pullout tray to retrofit a too-high surface.

The design of a new keyboard, mouse, or trackball may or may not reflect the influence of ergonomic scrutiny (see pages 114–115). If you use a pullout keyboard tray, make sure it can hold the mouse, too, so you won't have to constantly reach up to the desktop. Wrist rests, available for both keyboard and mouse use, help guide your position, but don't press down on them while working.

The chair. Choosing a desk chair is especially important, since you're likely to spend a lot of time in one. A chair with adjustable seat height will allow you to type efficiently as well as work comfortably at your desk. Arm rests should be adjustable and should not prevent you from pulling close into your desk or keyboard.

In good chairs you can change the cant of the seat to produce the most favorable hip-to-knee alignment. Support for your lumbar (lower spine) area is also important, so make sure that the chair firmly fits the small of your back. If necessary, use an adjustable foot rest to keep your feet flat on the floor.

And regardless of the chair, experts agree that you have to meet it halfway. Yes, your mother was right: sit up straight!

Your eyesight. To protect against eyestrain, a computer monitor should be located about 16 to 28 inches (or an arm's length) from the operator's face. Place the top of the monitor even with the top of your head, so that your eyes are aligned with the first few lines on the screen. (One exception: bifocal wearers should align the screen with their line of focus.) A copy holder or slantboard should be positioned at about the same distance as the monitor, slightly to one side or directly below.

As detailed on page 111, another source of eyestrain is the balance between light levels in the room and on your monitor. Adjust your screen illumination to match room lighting and turn the contrast up.

Glare is another big problem. It can come from overhead fixtures, a nearby task lamp, highly reflective surfaces, or a window in front of or behind you. If possible, place yourself at a 90° angle to a window or other bright light source. Screen shades or glare guards can help shield your monitor.

The near-reach zone. Although it's hard to accomplish, aim to place everything you need on a regular basis within arm's reach. If that's too tough, consider setting up multiple use areas and rolling your chair from zone to zone as required. A telephone headset helps relieve the stress of heavy phone use, especially while you're straining to find or do something else.

Break time. It's important to give yourself a break. Most experts believe that one of the major causes of repetitive stress injuries is the computer's mes-

An Ergonomic Overview

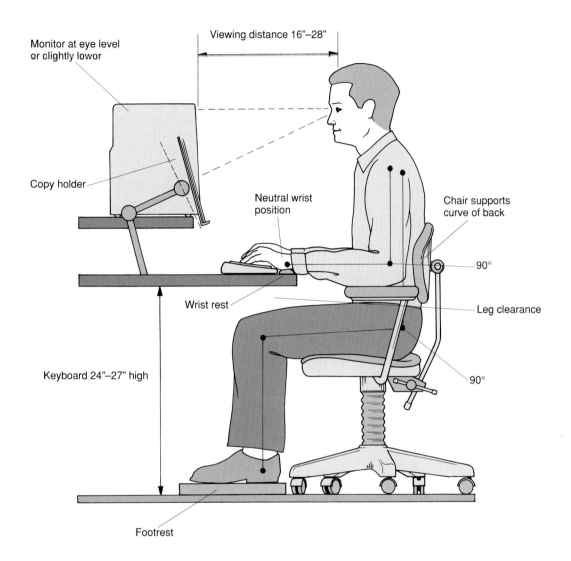

Monitor at eye level or slightly lower

Viewing distance 16"–28"

Copy holder

Neutral wrist position

Chair supports curve of back

90°

Leg clearance

Wrist rest

90°

Keyboard 24"–27" high

Footrest

merizing ability to allow work—and potentially damaging repetitive motion—to flow past the danger point.

Ergonomists recommend looking away from the computer screen and blinking hard at frequent intervals, getting up and stretching every 30 minutes, and taking a break each hour. Change your position frequently and plan your time so you can mix tasks. If you need a

reminder, you can find several software programs that will prompt you to relax at prescribed intervals—and even guide you through a refreshing exercise break. Or set the alarm on your computer to prompt you periodically.

Shopping for health. You'll find additional details on ergonomic products throughout "A Shopper's Guide," pages

91–125. Besides adjustable workstations and ergonomic chairs, look for articulating keyboard trays, monitor lifts, slantboards, adjustable keyboards, trackballs, wrist rests, footrests, and headsets. But remember that, just like "light" foods in the supermarket, so-called "ergonomic" products aren't certified. So shop from reputable sources and always ask to test any product before buying it.

Be sure to allow enough clearance between furnishings so you can maneuver easily. Also check to see that at least 36 inches of walking space is available for visitors and behind chairs. Walk through the motions you'll use in your new space, then mark traffic patterns and any potential problems on your plan.

GOING ELECTRONIC?

One reason for the home-office revolution is the advent of smaller, more affordable personal computers and other electronic aids once found only in commercial spaces. The box at right outlines some devices to consider. You probably won't need them all, but each one you select will have an impact on your space planning.

Turn back to pages 18–19 to review the ergonomic recommendations for a computer keyboard and monitor. When planning for a printer or copier, make allowances for both its bulk and its appetite for paper (and the way the paper feeds). Does your copier have a moving platen? If so, give it room. Can your printer go on a pullout shelf below the fax or answering machine?

Be sure to allow adequate space for air circulation and clearance for cords and cables. Shield computer components from direct sun. If on/off switches are located on the backs of machines, you may wish to install pullout shelves or swivels—or plug cords into switchable outlet strips or surge protectors (see page 119).

Shared-function machines such as telephone/fax/answering machines and printer/fax/copiers can save space, but research them carefully: they may lack the features, or the quality, of dedicated (single-purpose) components. Also take a look at voice-mail cards (page 124) and internal fax modems (pages 124–125) that let you "tuck" an on-counter machine into your personal computer.

The telephone is a home office lifeline, and its position should be planned carefully. Some experts recommend that, if you're right-handed, you place the phone near your left side as you sit at your desk. Then, if you jot on a pad as you talk, your right hand will be free and the cord won't pull across your body. If you're left-handed, reverse the position. To avoid being tied down, many office owners are switching to cordless models, which have recently improved in transmission quality.

THE ELECTRONIC OFFICE

Although the list is constantly changing, here's a sampling of electronic components you might find in a well-appointed home office. You probably won't want or need all this gear. Focus on your own specific needs, equipment budget, and available space.

For a detailed look at each product, see "A Shopper's Guide," pages 91–125.

- Desktop computer: monitor, CPU (central processing unit), keyboard, mouse, CD-ROM drive
- Notebook, subnotebook, or palmtop computer
- Laser, ink-jet, or dot-matrix printer
- Multi-line telephone, cordless phone or headset, cellular phone, pager
- Answering machine or voice-mail card
- Modem (internal or desktop)
- Fax machine (internal and/or desktop)
- Desktop copier
- Scanner

Mobile headsets (page 121) can free you to work with both hands.

Going online? Thinking of telecommuting? If so, it's important to figure your phone needs carefully. We've found that for those who frequently telecommute or network from home, even four phone lines are none too many—that's one personal line, one business line, one dedicated fax line, and one line linked to a modem. Add a second business line and a teenager's personal line, and you can see that things get complicated.

Multi-line telephones help; so do new home "switchboards" that allow you to cut off or redirect calls, dial from room to room, and add intercom and security channels to the phone system. But some things don't change: one designer reports that his dogs now bark when they hear the designated front-door "ring" from the phone—just as they once did for the doorbell.

One Wiring Scheme

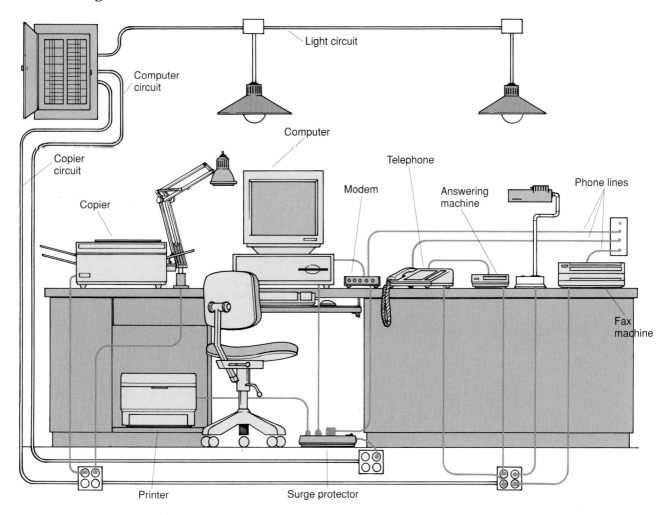

Light circuit

Computer circuit

Computer

Telephone

Copier circuit

Modem

Answering machine

Phone lines

Copier

Fax machine

Printer

Surge protector

GET WIRED

All those electronic options can pose new challenges for your home's electrical circuits. Be sure you have adequate power, evenly distributed among existing circuits; or plan to add additional circuits and/or a larger service entrance. For help with mapping your circuits, consult an electrician or see the *Sunset* book *Basic Wiring.*

Generally speaking, copiers pull the most power, with printers a distant second. If your lights flicker when the copier kicks on, you may have a problem. To safeguard stored data, don't plug another major component into the same circuit as your computer.

Starting from scratch? It's best to allow at least two dedicated 20-amp circuits for your office: one for the computer, printer, and peripherals and a second for a copier and other office equipment. It's

also best to place light fixtures on their own circuit, though it can also serve lights in another room.

Surge protectors (see page 119) help offset power spikes (increases in voltage) that could damage your computer's circuitry. For insurance, consider an uninterruptible power supply (UPS) that buys you several extra backup minutes if the power goes out. Don't rely on flimsy extension cords; instead, plan to add additional wall outlets and/or plug-in power strips.

Double-check requirements and routing logistics for phone lines, fax line, modem line, coaxial cable, intercom, and any remote audio/video systems you may be considering.

With all those cords and wires running amok, it's not surprising that a certain "spaghetti-wire syndrome" now menaces many home offices. Countertop grommets and cable raceways can tame these tangles; for details, see page 111.

THINK STORAGE

In a home office, the need for adequate storage is particularly acute. Without it, important documents, correspondence, and supplies can easily get mislaid, buried, bent, and dog-eared. Not to mention the time you'll waste looking for that note that was "right here a second ago."

If you're serious about keeping your office orderly, it's crucial to gain a sense of just how much storage space is necessary—and how much is simply an invitation to clutter. For step-by-step guidelines, see "Get Organized," below.

As you try to anticipate the amount of storage you'll need, think in generous terms. It's much more common to get into the bind of having too little storage than to have too much.

Make lists of what you need to store, right down to paper clips. Every kind of work has its own storage inventory, whether it's piles of periodicals for a writer or fabric and wallpaper samples for an interior designer.

Do pencils and stapler go on the work surface, on a nearby shelf, or into a shallow drawer or pull-out bin? What about stacking bins versus file draw-

GET ORGANIZED

The all-electronic revolution has yet to happen, and growing piles of correspondence, magazines, pencils, paper clips, and computer disks continue to bury many of us. Fortunately, there's help for those who want it from the growing ranks of designers who specialize in office planning. Here's a look at overall recommendations—some of them painful—they've put forth.

Make a list. To plan your storage needs, you must have an accurate picture of what materials are to be stored. Write down everything you plan to house in your office, from pencils and paper clips to research materials and file folders.

Next, make piles. Now comes the toughest part—going through both your list and your physical collections and actually deciding where things go.

Aim to sort office supplies, research materials, and odds and ends into four piles: 1) things you use daily; 2) things you use weekly; 3) things you'll

use within a month or two; and 4) things that, face it, you rarely or never use. Don't stop to read anything or spend a lot of time thinking about it, and don't put items aside to consider later (you won't).

Plan to place whatever you use daily within arm's reach. That doesn't necessarily mean on the desktop; it can go in a nearby drawer, shelf, or bin.

Store materials in the used-weekly pile elsewhere in the office. Items in the third pile may require hard decisions. For the fourth pile, the answer is simple: either recycle it or toss it (tax returns and other such records excepted). Experts concur: you must be especially ruthless at this point, or you'll lose whatever ground you've gained.

Magazines and newsletters can be stumbling blocks. Either place them in binders or vertical files on a shelf, or cut out or photocopy articles you intend to read and recycle the rest.

Tame those files. Filing systems require special handling.

The key is to get everything into a file folder and off the work surface. One filing system divides subjects into current, reference, and historical groupings. You'd use current files regularly, reference materials occasionally, and historical records once a year or so. Again, plan to make frequently used files immediately accessible; move rarely consulted records to a storage space outside of the office.

Devise some sort of coherent, flexible filing system, consisting of paper file folders within hanging folders inside a file cabinet, movable cabinet, or other suitable container. You could file hanging folders in alphabetical order, by broad subject, or numerically. The point is to come up with some order that allows you to retrieve items and, more important, to file and refile them instantly

Stacks of materials awaiting an executive decision spell trouble. If you must have a "holding tank," make it a set of compact stacking bins or another clearly defined zone; don't pile unat-

ers? Would movable files help you save steps and free up drawer space? Think of your work area as an airline cockpit: everything you need on a daily basis should be within easy reach—though not necessarily on the desk. Always ask yourself, "Does this really need to be in my office at all?"

Today's manufacturers offer a range of storage accommodations for everything from floppy disks to art boards. All you need to do is determine your needs and the available space. When shopping, you'll find a new range of styles and colors that say "home," not "office."

If you prefer to create your own storage style, you can use anything that works—from a steamer trunk for files to an umbrella stand for rolls of blueprints. Or try a bevy of baskets. One benefit of working at home is that you often enjoy a freer sense of office style.

Don't forget to look up. When some of us plan an office, we tend to fill up all the floor space and forget the verticals. Bookshelves, wall cabinets, pullouts, and floor-to-ceiling wall systems all help utilize above-desk space. For details, see pages 102–107.

tended-to items back on the desk or shove them into hiding in a file cabinet for later.

Get your life in order. According to home office designers, one reason we keep piles of paper around is that they remind us of things we're afraid we'll forget if they're out of sight. A final key to the clutter-free office is to replace these jumbles with a more organized personal system.

You can organize on paper or on the computer. Planning calendars can integrate appointments with your address book, contact list, and to-do notes. A growing amount of "personal organizing" computer software can do the same. Bulletin boards, blackboards, or white boards can record work flow and keep current concerns visible—though even these can harbor clutter if you're not careful.

Armed with a realistic plan for your storage needs, you can go back to blocking out space for storage units you actually need—rather than for furniture to simply hide junk.

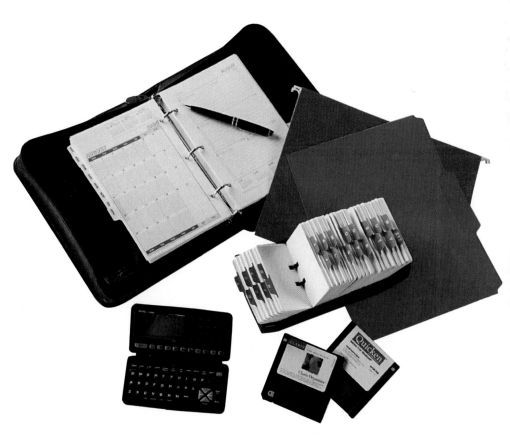

ADD LIGHT, NOT GLARE

Interior illumination comes from three different sources. Natural light (or daylight) floods into a room through windows and skylights. Depending on the orientation of these and the time of day, the season, and the weather—natural light can have either a gentle or harsh effect.

The other two kinds of light are artificial. When artificial light from a central source is diffused throughout a room and provides a uniform level of illumination, the effect is called ambient lighting. Artificial light that is concentrated and directed on a particular area is called task lighting. Whether or not an office has good natural light, it will need both types of artificial light.

Natural lighting. Windows, skylights, and French or sliding patio doors bring light, air, and views to your home office. The trick is to provide adequate natural light, but not too much.

Windows may be double-hung, casement, sliding, awning, hopper, or fixed in style. If in doubt, follow the styles used elsewhere in your house or neighborhood. What matters most is exposure: south windows let in bright, direct sun, while north windows provide soft, diffuse light. High clerestory windows and skylights draw light deeper into the room while maintaining privacy. Also consider glass block, which is making another comeback.

Think of French and sliding doors as windows, too: today they share the same solid construction and energy-efficient glazing. While hinged French doors mark the traditional indoor-outdoor transition, today's sliders seal better and can look great, too.

Ambient lighting. Creating soft ambient lighting for a home office requires careful planning. It's important to avoid high contrast between your work area and its surroundings. If you're working at a computer screen, for example, too little or too much background light will require your eyes to adjust frequently. A dimmer switch can control ambient lighting and add flexibility. Having several light sources is preferable to having just one.

Three Layers of Light

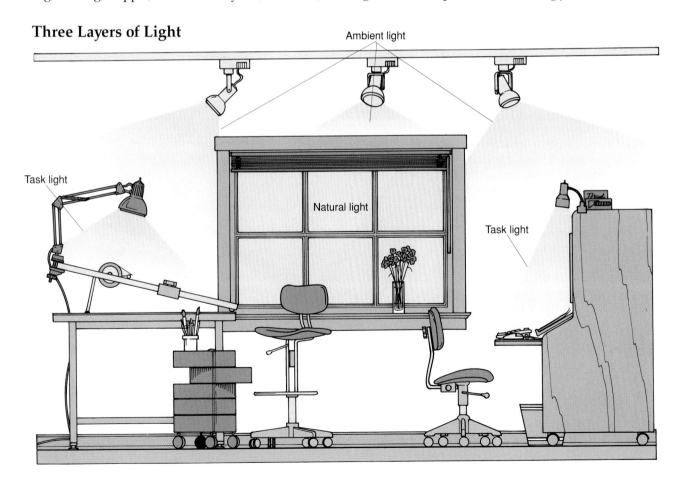

Ambient light

Task light

Natural light

Task light

Task lighting. Whether emitted from individual desk lamps or from track lights mounted on the ceiling or a wall, task lighting focuses illumination on areas where vision will be concentrated. Insufficient lighting can quickly lead to eyestrain.

If you're right-handed, task lighting should shine over your left shoulder so that your writing won't cast shadows on your work. If you're left-handed, it should shine over your right shoulder. Keep in mind, too, that a desk lamp with a fluorescent tube will not cast a shadow like that of a lamp with an incandescent or halogen bulb.

Beware of glare. Besides inadequate lighting, glare must also be assiduously avoided. Office lighting designs evolved for paper-related tasks, but the computer has changed all that. In general, computer environments require lower levels of well-shielded ambient light than traditional offices plus flexible task lighting that can be tailored to the job at hand. If possible, place both ambient and task fixtures on dimmer switches.

Computer users know how glare detracts from the visibility of a monitor screen. Glare is commonly produced in three ways: 1) light bulbs are reflected on the screen from above and behind the computer operator; 2) bright windows are situated behind the screen; and 3) shiny surfaces within the user's field of vision compete with the screen. Window coverings (pages 28–29) can help; so can a screen shade or glare guard for your monitor.

PRESERVE THE PEACE

As they say, the best guardian of office privacy is an office door that closes—preferably a solid door, not a thin, hollow-core model. Built-in cabinets, dividers, and fabric screens not only promote privacy and mark off space, but also help baffle sound.

And think about surfaces. Thick carpeting goes a long way toward minimizing noise reflection. Acoustic ceiling tiles help, too; if you don't like their appearance, you can get out your staple gun and cover them with fabric—for a custom decor and even more insulation. Fiberglass or rigid-board insulation can help, as can double- or triple-glazed windows and patio doors. If sound remains a problem, designers recommend doubling the ceiling or walls and sandwiching dead space or extra insulation between the two layers.

But for some people, having too little noise can be as distracting as having too much. Low-volume classical music, environmental tapes, or even "white-noise" sounds can generate enough background noise to go almost unnoticed while masking the sounds of computer or printer. One home-based business writer installed an old-fashioned ceiling fan to improve air flow in his second-story office—and found that the soft, tropical whir of its blades supplied just enough background noise to improve his concentration.

HEAT IT UP, COOL IT DOWN

Insufficient climate control may not seem important until you log several winter or summer work sessions in your new space. But either heat or cold can be a major source of restlessness, irritability, and lack of productivity. You shouldn't have to dress in down booties and scratchy long johns to work at home in December or peel down to swimsuit and thongs in August.

If you use a computer and live in an area where temperatures are very high, air-conditioning may be necessary no matter where your office is located—for the protection of delicate computer files as well as for your comfort.

Be sure to determine whether your present heating and cooling system can provide sufficient climate control for your new office. If not, can you simply reroute existing ductwork (avoiding having any direct heat source near your computer), or will you have to upgrade or add an auxiliary unit?

Also plan for adequate air circulation. Well-placed windows, operable skylights, and fans help move air, but make sure they won't blow your papers around, too.

ADD AMENITIES

Will you need space for conference seating? If so, be sure to allow 36 inches for traffic flow around the table.

What about an overstuffed chair or couch for reading, contemplation, or a break from keyboarding? How about a snack bar? Want to lower stress by watching colorful fish flicker past in a built-in tank? Maybe you'd like shelves for stereo speakers, or display niches for an art collection? Sketch the possibilities onto your hand-drawn plan.

SETTING A STYLE

Once the functional pieces fit, step back and consider how your office design will look. Not only will the right surroundings spur you on psychologically, but appearance will also count when you host clients or friends.

From leather briefcases to computer hardware, many business accoutrements have a uniform look. But in your home office, you can express your own tastes and individuality. And since manufacturers are beginning to target office products specifically to the home market, you now have more choices than ever before.

But having an office at home also makes you responsible for more than style. You need to consider upkeep, safety, and general durability. In addition to enjoying the fun of selecting your favorite look, you'll also have to come to terms with costs.

Start with the photographs in this book. Look carefully at the installations that appeal to you the most, then try to analyze what it is about them that you like. Take notes about colors, fabrics, and accessories, and supplement them with pictures you've clipped from magazines, catalogs, and advertising supplements.

If possible, visit decorators' showrooms and furniture stores. Try to identify specific products, designers, and other sources for the look you'd like to achieve. If you need additional help, you'll find a list of professional resources on page 27.

DECIDING ON COLORS

The colors traditionally used in offices have been muted ones. With the exception of certain creative fields, the business world apparently runs more smoothly in an environment of calm, neutral tones, such as beiges and grays.

Look around the other rooms of your house to help you choose the colors with which you feel most at ease. Whether you favor earth tones, crayon colors, soft pastels, bold contrasts, or delicate harmonies, you can probably carry a similar theme into your office. You may notice that certain rooms have a more relaxed ambience, while others, decorated in more lively colors, are more challenging in feeling. An office should provide a relaxed environment that also stimulates energy, so a balance between quiet and more vibrant colors may be best.

Remember, too, that color is mercurial, looking subtly to sharply different as surroundings change and light varies. You would probably choose different shades of blue for your office depending on whether the predominant daylight was sunny or overcast. The type of light fixture and bulb you use (see pages 108–111) can also affect how colors look.

Deep or bright colors make a small room seem smaller. White or very pale colors can lend an illusion of greater size.

Color Wheel

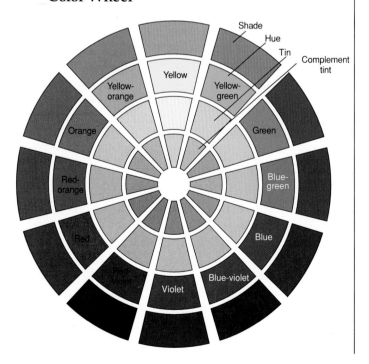

The color wheel (see facing page) can help you choose compatible hues for your palette. Colors that face each other across the color wheel, such as yellow and violet, are called complementary. Placed together, they create a strong contrast that's exciting to some tastes, disturbing to others. Harmonious colors, on the other hand, represent a continuous segment of the color wheel. They produce gentle color gradations—blue to blue-violet to violet, for example.

Any color can vary in value, becoming more pastel with the addition of white or deeper with the addition of black. While black and white are not colors, both, along with gray (a mixture of the two), can provide striking contrasts for color accents.

FLOOR COVERINGS

Though rarely noticed consciously, the floor covering often sets the mood of a room by virtue of its design, texture, and color. A wide range of materials is available, including wood, resilient vinyl and rubber, ceramic tile, masonry, and carpeting. Not all serve a home office equally well; the more you can narrow down the choices before you shop, the easier your final decision will be.

Besides appearance and maintenance, consider noise; the right floor covering can help soundproof an office. If this is a concern, your best bet is to choose a soft material that absorbs sound, such as vinyl, rubber, or carpeting.

Next consider wear. Though an office usually gets less traffic than other areas of the house, you'll probably want to invest in a floor covering that will last for many years. Industrial- or commercial-grade carpeting, level-loop carpeting, and studded or ribbed rubber flooring are good choices. Office-supply stores sell transparent mats of rigid plastic to protect carpet and wood floors under desk and chair areas, where wear is constant.

If your work requires you to be on your feet for long periods of time, comfort should be a high-priority item. Most comfortable underfoot are soft and resilient floor coverings—carpeting, rubber, and vinyl.

Care of a wood floor involves more fuss than care of most resilient floor coverings or carpeting. If your job involves the use of chemicals, paints, or

NEED HELP?

Many of us lack either the energy or the expertise to tackle a major remodeling project from start to finish. Fortunately, help is available. The listing below describes design professionals and points out the differences among them.

Architects. Architects are state-licensed professionals with degrees in architecture. They're trained to create designs that are structurally sound, functional, and aesthetically pleasing. They know construction materials, can negotiate bids from contractors, and can supervise the work. If stress calculations must be made, architects can make them; other professionals (such as designers and contractors) need a state-licensed engineer to design the structure and sign the working drawings.

Interior designers. Even if you're working with an architect, you may wish to call on the services of an interior designer for finishing touches. Designers and decorators specialize in decorating and furnishing rooms and can offer fresh, innovative ideas and advice. Through their contacts, a homeowner has access to materials and products not available at the retail level.

Office designers. As home design becomes more sophisticated, professionals become more specialized. Though office designers in the past were engaged to plan large commercial spaces, a new breed specializes in home offices. Like interior designers, office designers understand and have access to the latest materials and products.

Other specialists. Showroom personnel, furniture-store salespeople, office-warehouse or building-center staff, and other retailers can help you choose and, in some cases, combine components to create a home office that's right for you. In fact, this kind of help may be all you need if your requirements are minor. For a larger job, check the specialist's qualifications carefully. Ask if you may visit or see photos of completed installations. Though some salespeople are quite capable and helpful, others may be motivated simply to sell you more goods or a particular line of products.

other liquids, you'll want a flooring that cleans up quickly and easily, such as tile or resilient vinyl. Concrete is popular in large studios; when laid over radiant heating coils, concrete slabs can feel surprisingly cozy.

WALL COVERINGS

As with floor coverings, wall coverings come in a broad range of styles and a wide variety of materials. In selecting one for your home office, you'll need to balance aesthetics with practicality.

You can paint the walls in a solid color or in a design, or you can use wallpaper, which offers a kaleidoscope of colors, textures, and patterns.

Another option is wood paneling. It creates a cozy, warm atmosphere in the tradition of a den or study. But beware of using dark wood in a dimly lit room—the effect will be to make the room darker and smaller-looking.

Sometimes the right wall covering can assist you in your work. Walls of cork double as bulletin boards and offer the additional advantage of muffling sound. Or tuck blackboards or white boards between countertops and overhead shelves.

WINDOW COVERINGS

If you're lucky enough to have a window with a view and if privacy isn't a problem, you may want to leave the window uncovered. But the need to control natural light may be more important than preserving the view. At certain times of day, intensive, angled sunlight can become an office nuisance—even making work temporarily impossible. The right window covering can temper such interference.

ARCHITECT: REMICK ASSOCIATES ARCHITECTS-BUILDERS, INC.

INTERIOR DESIGNER: AGNES BOURNE, INC.

Soft window coverings—curtains and drapes, or shades made of canvas or fabric—are reassuringly familiar to us. But, while attractive in domestic interiors, soft curtains may clutter an office, especially if they have lots of folds and frills. Fabric shades, though less intrusive, allow little flexibility: rolled up, they may let in too much light; pulled down, they block it completely.

Hard window coverings, such as adjustable miniblinds and louvered shutters, offer the greatest control over both privacy and sunlight. They stay neatly in place and give your office a more tailored look. White and lightly tinted treatments retain heat less than dark colors, a welcome feature on warm summer days.

Office styles run the gamut from traditional (facing page) through Southwestern (below) to colorfully eclectic (right).

DESIGN: THOMAS CALLAWAY

ARCHITECT: BRIAN BRAND/BAYLIS BRAND WAGNER ARCHITECTS. INTERIOR DESIGNER: R.W. BURTON DESIGNS

GREAT HOME OFFICES

We've examined the basic building blocks. Now it's time for some graphic inspiration. This chapter showcases what could be termed "self-contained" offices. We begin with "Specialized Spaces," featuring a baker's dozen of beautiful rooms that paint a broad band of possibilities. "Lofts & Landings" explores the virtues of going up—and out. And "The Backyard Commute" takes a look at everyone's dream office, the detached cottage or studio.

Some views here are grand; some offices are frankly architectural. Others were carved from small guest rooms or landings. We've tried to demonstrate the diversity of office styles and shapes out there—and to show that today's designs don't look just like offices, they look like homes. Don't worry if your available space or budget doesn't seem to fit the bill; many of these ideas can be scaled down effectively.

This elegant office forms a self-contained "flight room" for two pilots, housing his-and-her oak desks, under-counter fridge, and discreet computer, audio, and home-security gear—mostly behind trim cabinet doors. There's room to spare for a comfortable sitting area and gas fireplace.

SPECIALIZED SPACES

INTERIOR DESIGNER: VAN-MARTIN ROWE INTERIOR DESIGN STUDIO

*Created from a spare bedroom, this classic U-shaped layout (facing page) is
built from solid, edge-joined oak that's been lightly pickled. An open counter
and keyboard pullout provide a comfortable workstation for a resident screen-
writer, and the spacious, overhanging peninsula allows room to spread out
drafts and research notes. A curved daybed (below) rests under handsome
shelves that seem to float unsupported. What's the secret? The
massive-looking units are actually hollow, slipping over steel rods
that extend from wall studs behind.*

*Let a home office express your style! Revealing an energetic splash of shapes
and colors, this interior designer's office entices guests and clients from just
off an entry hallway. The black-and-white spaniel makes its own contribu-
tion to an already exuberant design scheme.*

INTERIOR DESIGNER: BAUER INTERIOR DESIGN

SPECIALIZED
SPACES

This library speaks volumes: it's the working retreat of an historian and professor of economics. Paired walls the width of a library carrel (near right) provide a decompression zone between the inner office (facing page) and adjacent rooms. A tall arch marks one wall of the bookish pair, a freestanding gabled pediment the other.

The desk-and-credenza idea may be traditional, but this elegant office is anything but stuffy. The overall look invokes trim, Eurostyle efficiency, with balanced illumination from recessed downlights, a deskside pendant, and natural daylight. Custom cabinets are faced with purple-heart and ebony; kickspaces below cabinets sport hidden strip lights—just for fun.

INTERIOR DESIGNER: RUTH LIVINGSTON

ARCHITECT: MUI HO

ARCHITECT: GEORGE SUYAMA ARCHITECTS

Like a space-within-a-space, a self-contained office (above) fits under part of a vaulted living room (facing page). When it's time for work, the oak office doors slide shut, revealing handsome built-in bookcases. From the desk, the view is through an inner glazed window, past the dining room, and through an exterior window wall to the waterfront beyond. This office serves two other functions, too: it's a bedroom for visiting grandchildren (there's a pull-down Murphy bed in one wall), and—with doors opened wide—it becomes a serving station when the owners entertain.

A his-and-hers corridor office, wrapped in traditional walnut, has built-in custom counters and glass-fronted wall units. Beyond, a shelf-flanked Palladium window beckons with an inviting bench.

ARCHITECT: J. ALLEN SAYLES

SPECIALIZED

SPACES

INTERIOR DESIGNER: SHARON CAMPBELL, ASID

One half of a two-story addition, this downstairs office provides plenty of elbow room in the form of twin U-shaped layouts (left). Counter materials join wire-mesh safety glass to laminated layers of 13-ply maple plywood; frames and end panels are steel. An adjacent "file room" (below) features banks of recessed cabinets, ample counter space, and sturdy bookshelves suspended on industrial threaded rods and steel U-channels. A wall unit's oak doors (right) flip up to reveal phone books—plus a splash of purple dye stain.

SPECIALIZED
SPACES

INTERIOR DESIGNER: SALLY SIRKIN LEWIS INTERIOR DESIGN.
CUSTOM FURNITURE: SALLY SIRKIN LEWIS / J. ROBERT SCOTT & ASSOCIATES, INC.

A gentleman's study is handsomely appointed with a walnut desk and side chairs at one end (facing page) and a comfortable conversation space at the other (below); a cozy fireplace (not shown) lies between. Double doors open onto the adjacent living room or close for privacy. Built-in bookcases, like the paneled wainscoting, are of oak. A large domed central skylight crowns the room.

A great home gym meets a great home office, mixing aerobics and electronics in one space. The main room was originally a bedroom. Its ceiling was raised, a wall-to-wall mirror and exercise bar were installed, and a treadmill, bike, and incline board joined the black-lacquered desk. An adjacent closet was the shell for a fabric-lined addition, complete with phone and fax, bookshelves, file drawers, and a leather-topped work surface.

INTERIOR DESIGNER: ERIKA BRUNSON DESIGN ASSOCIATES

Twin rooftop towers house two wings of an architects' office, which floats atop an ultra-modern hillside house. The main room (left) features ample work counters, flat files, and storage cubbies, all sprayed with granite-like atomizing paint. The view from this space leads across a slate-paved deck toward the other tower's striking galvanized siding (below). Amenities in this room (right) include a custom wall unit, a conference table, colorful 12-inch tiles, and a view back to the first tower's facade. Steel sliding doors open to a cantilevered deck with ocean views.

ARCHITECT: CIGOLLE + COLEMAN ARCHITECTS

*"Counter space and book space"
were what one computer pioneer
demanded of his upstairs office. The
long, corridor-style layout (right)
has continuous countertops on one
side and floor-to-ceiling bookcases
on the other. Wall cases above the
windows maximize soffit space and
house task lights (above).*

ARCHITECT: SANBORN DESIGNS INCORPORATED

DESIGN: ROBERT H. WATERMAN / WATERMAN & SUN

*A private retreat is accessed through
an adjacent master bedroom, which
serves as a buffer zone between
work and household. Knotty-pine
paneling, floral wallpaper, and wick-
er furnishings give a look of old-
fashioned ease. A ceiling fan adds air
circulation and another touch of the
timeless.*

The atmosphere needn't be workaholic: some people function better in a looser environment, surrounded by all their eclectic passions. Fly-tying gear, a rod and reel collection, old hand tools, and a mix of memorabilia surround the oak desk shown below, their histories adding comfort to a home office.

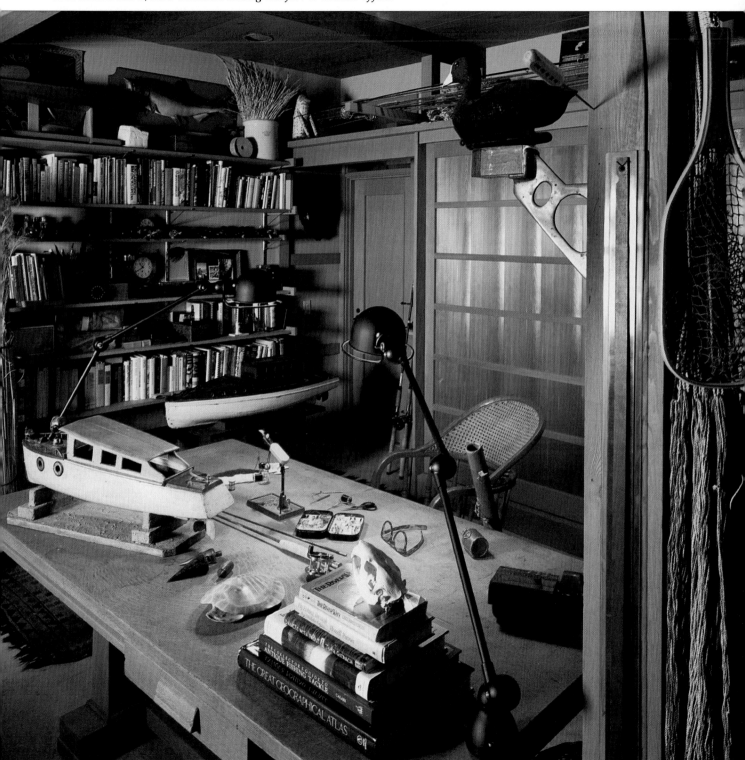

ARCHITECT: GEORGE SUYAMA ARCHITECTS

LOFTS & LANDINGS

Landings, whether minimalist or Colonial, can provide unique work spaces for those who like the mix of openness and privacy. This rebuild in a fire zone punctuates noncombustible materials—concrete, cement-panel walls, and structural steel—with bright, sculptural detailing. The glass-block ceiling admits light from a pocket deck above the compact office space.

DESIGN: BUFF, SMITH & HENSMAN ARCHITECTS/BOB MOORE DESIGN

An angular, second-story landing (above) projects an open office out over the living room and toward broad city views. The work layout (left) includes symmetrical his-and-her counters of burgundy-colored laminate and a central peninsula of glass. The computer's monitor pivots so keyboard and mouse can be shared. During construction, the builders routed a raceway through the floor to the opposite side of the office, allowing cords for fax, printers, and network peripherals to be placed across the room without exposing wires.

ARCHITECT: IAN FILLINGER/SAVIDGE WARREN + FILLINGER ARCHITECTS

LOFTS &
LANDINGS

ARCHITECT: CARRASCO & ASSOCIATES

"A New York loft" was the dream of a California homeowner—and this West Coast home office was the result. Tall posts, bolted to a sturdy ridge beam, provide anchor points for framing a loft with plenty of room for a desk, files, credenza, wall cabinet, and easel. Loft dwellers can take advantage of unused vertical space while keeping tabs on both dinner and family below.

A landing near the master bedroom makes a workable retreat for a marketing writer who likes to work at night without disturbing the household. Faux-marble paint and plate glass on the pivoting desk and matching wall unit echo bedroom furnishings beyond; cushy carpeting flows seamlessly from space to space.

INTERIOR DESIGNER: ROBERT SCOTT CATES/N.L. TOBIASON INTERIOR DESIGN

INTERIOR DESIGN: VAN-MARTIN ROWE INTERIOR DESIGN STUDIO

Interior windows give this octagonal office a view over the children's play area. The office, accessed via an open stairway and landing (above), is also the portal to a master suite beyond. Zigzagging maple counters (left) soften transitions, play off other angles, and step up to a 42-inch-tall equipment counter. Square panes in the skylight vault open hopper-style, bringing air and light to the north-facing room.

What if your home office outgrows its allotted space? Try breaking it up. The library on the facing page spreads around a remodeled landing leading from downstairs to the master bedroom. The bend in the landing forms an intimate book nook where one can study, browse, or simply gaze out through the peaked window wall to greenery beyond.

ARCHITECT: LUTHER M. HINTZ, AIA. INTERIOR DESIGNER: PAMELA PEARCE DESIGN

THE BACKYARD COMMUTE

This detached cottage, about a 30-second stroll from the main house, serves both as a home office and as guest quarters. On one side of its layout is a kitchenette. On the other, behind a divider wall, is a built-in desk backed by mirrored doors that slide open to reveal four lateral files, a small personal copier, and a constantly busy fax machine.

This 220-square-foot shack probably started out as a bunkhouse, but with the discreet addition of a salvaged steel window wall, a skylight, some laid-back interior changes, and a desk, it's become the light-filled home office of an architect.

DESIGN: BUFF, SMITH & HENSMAN ARCHITECTS / DESIGN AUTHOR CAROL SOUCEK KING

ARCHITECT: ROBERT MARQUIS

INTERIOR DESIGNER: HELEN L. CARREKER, ASID

An unneeded pool house became the setting for this self-contained office. A built-in room divider placed along the long axis creates a strip-layout work center (above) on one side, with a laminate-covered counter laid on top of lateral files. (These are lower than typical files—about 24½ inches tall—allowing a comfortable work surface above.) Storage abounds in both the divider wall and the handsome file units beyond. Turn a corner and you see the built-in conversation area (left). A mini-kitchen lies just beyond.

THE BACKYARD

COMMUTE

In a quiet and woodsy setting, the side-yard structure shown below is a peaceful place for a graphic artist to work. It's equipped with laminate counters and an open peninsula (right), storage closets with sliding mirrored doors, and crisp track lighting. The peninsula's back panels house wiring. They look great when closed (bottom left), even when reflected in adjacent mirrors. To access wire connections, one panel end pivots inside the groove in a floor-anchored cleat; friction pins hold the top in place.

ARCHITECT: BUFF, SMITH & HENSMAN ARCHITECTS

DESIGN: ROCKWOOD DESIGN & JUDITH MARSHALL

It's like a big backyard barn, but better. The main room (facing page) houses all the supplies—plus work in progress—of a working artist. A central island moves on wheels; clerestory windows and barn-style doors bring in classic northern studio light. An auxiliary office space (left) features a storage loft accessed by a sturdy ladder that runs back and forth in a wooden track. In fair weather, the telescoping exterior "walls" slide in channels to open to the outdoors (above). When things turn nasty, radiant-heat coils embedded in the studio's concrete floor help dry both artist and artwork.

INTERIOR DESIGNER: OSBURN DESIGN

FOUND-SPACE SOLUTIONS

By now, you've seen some great self-contained offices. Here the focus shifts to shared spaces, the bottom line for those of us who just don't have the opportunity or desire for a separate room. But even though we call these "found-space solutions," we think you'll agree that they're no less sensational than the offices shown in "Great Home Offices," pages 31–57.

We begin the tour with the bedroom office, a prime option for the space-deprived. Then it's on to living rooms, dining rooms, kitchens, and closets. Attics, basements, and garages present special office opportunities, though renovating them can be hard work. And don't overlook porches and pop-outs. Throughout, the emphasis is on space-saving tricks, flexibility, and design touches that will make your shared space as hard-working and attractive as it can be.

A basement closet takes on a colorful new life as an office alcove. And even though it's small, it has room for the basics: drafting board, phone, files, and track lights. Both bookcase and countertop were shaped from inexpensive fiberboard that's bullnosed up front.

THE BEDROOM OFFICE

A 6- by 8-foot office L, built from leather-topped bird's-eye maple, occupies one corner of the master bedroom, providing a tranquil but efficient workstation for a busy traveling executive. Note how the desk's color and shape tactfully echo those of the bed and built-in headboard.

ARCHITECT: FRANK ISRAEL

These two work areas are apart—but not closed off—from adjacent rooms. At top, a decidedly modern master suite links an office alcove to a sitting room and bath; textured concrete, copper accents, and tightly woven wool carpet complete the picture. At bottom, the remodeled pop-out allowed just enough space for a built-in office alcove; laminate countertops and wall-hung bookcases maximize work space behind low knee walls.

ARCHITECT: REMICK ASSOCIATES ARCHITECTS-BUILDERS, INC.

ARCHITECT: CODY ASSOCIATES

FOUND-SPACE SOLUTIONS **61**

THE BEDROOM
OFFICE

DESIGN: DIANE CLOOS

Clutter-busting schemes for small bedrooms include fold-down Murphy beds and freestanding storage units that open up for work. Matching secretarials flanking a doorway (below) house workstations inside and appear almost sculptural when closed. The Murphy bed (at right) is part of a hard-working guest room/library combination.

ARCHITECT: TOM KUNDIG/ OLSON SUNDBERG

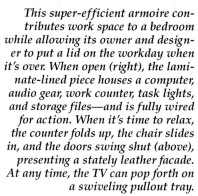

ARCHITECT: SANBORN DESIGNS INCORPORATED

This super-efficient armoire contributes work space to a bedroom while allowing its owner and designer to put a lid on the workday when it's over. When open (right), the laminate-lined piece houses a computer, audio gear, work counter, task lights, and storage files—and is fully wired for action. When it's time to relax, the counter folds up, the chair slides in, and the doors swing shut (above), presenting a stately leather facade. At any time, the TV can pop forth on a swiveling pullout tray.

ARCHITECT: SANBORN DESIGNS INCORPORATED

INTERIOR DESIGNER: AMOROSO/HOLMAN DESIGN GROUP

Kids' rooms often need surfaces for study. Colorful built-ins energize an eight-year-old's domain (above), while a laminate countertop under the window maximizes work space and minimizes mess. A split-level desk (left) built with unpeeled hickory uprights makes a neat homework corner in another room. And the teen "study" (right) has a wall unit an industrial-minded extraterrestrial might fancy: its adjustable shelves and panels are recycled plastic fastened to commercial steel U-channels. The rolling work table supports a growing electronic arsenal.

INTERIOR DESIGNER: MARC MELVIN/AGNES BOURNE, INC.

LIVING ROOMS

A small urban condominium must maximize space, and this one integrates his-and-hers offices, an art gallery, and a comfortable living room all in one. Moving back from a red-leather work table, the office steps up and past a vivid full-wall mural to a second work alcove with rolltop desk and shelving. Adjustable track fixtures provide both task lighting and accents for artwork. Not only does this living room look great, but its color scheme matches that of the outside view—part of an historic downtown district.

ARCHITECT: JIM OLSON / OLSON SUNDBERG ARCHITECTS

LIVING
ROOMS

INTERIOR DESIGNER: VAN-MARTIN ROWE INTERIOR DESIGN STUDIO

ARCHITECT: KOTAS-PANTALEONI ARCHITECTS

While some need a defined area for work, these office owners don't. A movie producer prefers the work zone formed by a modern cousin to the rolltop desk (above). The family-room alcove (lower right) was fashioned from a wet bar; the former bartop hides clutter while maintaining a link with clients and family. The towering steel book wall (upper right) houses an important collection of maritime books, while doubling as a living-room focal point; its industrial shelves are so strong that their owner simply climbs them, ladder-style, to find needed volumes.

DESIGN: SHARON SISTINE

A simple, waxed-pine farm table looks right at home in this living room and provides ample surface for work materials. The step-down from the main living room adds just enough separation to define the work area. The attraction of this layout is flexibility: the owner has a separate office elsewhere, but likes to move around the house as light and inspiration beckon.

INTERIOR DESIGNER: NICK BERMAN

INTERIOR DESIGNER: GARY HUTTON DESIGN

Taking the "live/work" option to its logical conclusion, this loft/warehouse layout mixes it all together: living room, office, conference area, bedroom, and kitchen. If you don't need strict privacy, this scheme allows some stimulating design options. Note here how visual barriers help break up space and indicate the boundaries of different zones.

"Where's the office?" we asked. "You're standing in it," the owner replied. She and her designer decided that all she really needed was an inconspicuous corner. At eye level, her desk is hidden by the couch (our camera was placed higher to reveal it). And where would the clunky, floor-model copier go? She tucked it behind a two-sided paper screen, adding a decorative uplight for accent.

INTERIOR DESIGNER: VAN-MARTIN ROWE INTERIOR DESIGN STUDIO

DINING ROOMS

In this hardworking, high-rise condo, every-thing disappears behind doors, including the dining-room office. The owners wanted what they needed nearby, but didn't want to look at it. The answer: good organization, efficient built-ins, and doors that slide completely out of the way on Eurostyle "flipper-door" hardware. The adjacent dining-room table doubles as a work surface, and dining chairs can become conference chairs.

ARCHITECT: OLSON SUNDBERG ARCHITECTS

INTERIOR DESIGNER: GEORGIA JOHNSTONE DESIGNS, INC.

After several years and long hours in a staff-filled office, this designer moved home, cut her overhead, and was able to integrate her daily life with work. Dining-room antiques (above) include an 18th-century plank table that doubles as work surface and conference table; a ship captain's rolltop desk with plenty of pigeon-holes; and an English pine wardrobe that houses office supplies, fax, and items that once required four separate cabinets. Phone time, typing, and paperwork spill over into the kitchen (left); in summer months, desk work and client meetings also spread to the nearby patio and garden.

KITCHENS

ARCHITECT: SANBORN DESIGNS INCORPORATED

Recycled hotel cubbyholes gain new life in the cheery breakfast area above. The wood unit, which benefited from a few timely repairs, is snugged between a glass-fronted kitchen cabinet and a white laminate built-in that holds both file drawers and a pop-up TV.

ARCHITECT: MULDER/KATKOV ARCHITECTURE

A mother and set designer needed a work space that would allow her to keep an eye on both dinner and her energetic offspring. The answer was a bank of built-ins made from the same maple as the kitchen cabinets and living-room units beyond. A sewing machine and typewriter (shown at left) pull out beyond base cabinets, ready for action.

KITCHENS

ARCHITECT: HOUSE + HOUSE OF SAN FRANCISCO. INTERIOR DESIGN: OSBURN DESIGN

ARCHITECT: GARY EARL PARSONS

Tucked in behind the refrigerator, this compact command center includes maple storage niches, black-stained ash drawers, and a cantilevered, angled maple desk complete with pencil groove—reminiscent of a country school desk.

A tailored kitchen work center fits seamlessly into the main cabinet run, allowing space for phone calls, correspondence, note-taking, and meal planning. Just beyond, in an adjacent room, lies the main home office.

An open floor plan, joining kitchen to living room, includes a "landing zone" for kitchen tasks and desk work. The kitchen features oak woodwork and sponge-painted concrete countertops. Pullouts minimize the desk's impact while adding efficiency; a half-wall divider hides clutter and offers a subtle sense of separation from the spaces beyond.

INTERIOR DESIGNER: MONROE & COMPANY

FOUND-SPACE SOLUTIONS **77**

CLOSETS

DESIGN: PAT & HOWARD CLARK

They raided an adjacent hall closet, removed its back wall, and used the resulting alcove to house a compact computer center for an existing office. The handsome workstation's file drawers are open on the side, allowing a seated user easy access.

This 56-square-foot utility closet has undergone some big changes. First they hid the water heater and cleaning supplies; then in came U-shaped counters and built-ins, a pullout cart, and some under-cabinet lighting. Note: for extended use, consider a neutral (not a banked) keyboard position as shown on page 19.

INTERIOR DESIGNER: HELEN L. CARREKER, ASID

INTERIOR DESIGNER: OSBURN DESIGN

The curved coat room beside a staircase lent just enough space for a ship-tight office. The family's multimedia computer rests atop a laminate countertop that continues the stairway's curve—and helps ease traffic through the narrow doorway. Finishing touches help stretch visual impact.

CLOSETS

INTERIOR DESIGNER: GREGORY VALERIO

Behind the shelves, there's a surprise: piano-hinged bookcases swing aside on casters, exposing an office. The T-shaped desktop folds down from wall shelves; a fluorescent tube is mounted below the cabinet. With the office closed up, an adjacent unit opens to reveal a media center.

DESIGN: TERRY ANNE MECKLER AND JAMES VOGLER

They found space beneath the stairs—enough space, that is, for a computer, a work counter, and some office supplies. A tambour front conceals this under-stair workstation when it's not in use.

A converted closet in the den (below) sports a track-lit reference wall over an ample computer desk flanked by file cabinets. The keyboard slides out on a modified top drawer, and the printer rolls out from the desk's kneehole. The desk sits on casters to keep access to wiring easy. When everything is tucked back in, bifold doors conceal it all.

DESIGN: RICHARD WATSON

Can you keep a secret? One section of this living-room bookcase swings open to reveal a fully outfitted office that occupies under-stair space. For quiet and security, the soundproof room can be locked up tight.

DESIGN: BARBARA AND GENTRY WADE

FOUND-SPACE SOLUTIONS **81**

ATTICS, BASEMENTS, GARAGES

ARCHITECT: WILLIAM CURTIS AND PATRICIA EMMONS

Baskets and built-ins give a crisp look to a bright, white attic office (facing page) formed from a tiny bedroom and laundry room. Cubbyhole cases follow the roof pitch. Skylight, track fixtures, and under-cabinet fluorescents balance light in a naturally dim space.

Away from roof peaks, attic ceilings can get low fast. The design shown above brought all the standing and circulation functions out into the center of the room and relegated sitting and storage areas to the sides. Running along each low wall is a continuous counter. The attic at right makes a virtue out of awkward roof angles, highlighting them with impeccable ceiling paneling and trim.

ARCHITECT: REMICK ASSOCIATES ARCHITECTS-BUILDERS, INTERIOR DESIGNER: ALICE WILEY INTERIOR DESIGN

ATTICS, BASEMENTS, GARAGES

Daylit basements can offer valuable office space and needn't be dreary. The compact architect's office at right opens to a backyard view and fits four drawing tables around a central conference table. A second basement office, shown below, is comprised of several linked use areas (they grew as business grew) and features a stylish conference area brightened with sponge-painted walls and halogen bounce lighting.

ARCHITECT: THOMAS L. BOSWORTH, FAIA

INTERIOR DESIGN: OSBURN DESIGN

DESIGN: JAMES E. BOLEN INTERIOR PLANNING & DESIGN

*Basement built-ins—from counters and cabinets to an art wall—warm this
potentially "cold" space with glowing wood tones. Custom pieces were built
from maple plywood faced with solid lumber; they're playfully oriented at
angles to walls, and offer a plethora of pullouts and other space-saving touches.
A couch adds a sense of comfort to any office space.*

ARCHITECT: BOYD/JENKS ASSOCIATES

The bright artist's studio at left, with its 18-foot-high ceiling and ridge skylight, has the look of an English cottage, but it grew out of a small, dark garage (now home to a printing press). An 18- by 18-foot extension to the existing structure provided the artist with the extra space to paint, as well as with garden views and a small bath. The studio addition, shown above (near the wood pile), pushes out at the end of the garage. A shed-roofed extension (with low skylights) marks the bathroom's location.

Functional flexibility, in both furniture and organization, distinguishes the redesign of a daylit basement in a hillside house. The owners wanted to replace three small bedrooms with two home offices that could also serve as sleeping quarters for guests. One side of each rolling storage cabinet is hinged and folds down to become a temporary desk. Custom-designed shoji panels—made of wood and sandblasted glass—follow the lines of the old interior walls, making it possible to keep the space open or divide it.

PORCHES & POP-OUTS

DESIGN: ALAN JENCKS

An office in a redwood forest? The eclectic three-story addition at the rear of this house (facing page) features a master bedroom with sliding wall and sleeping deck; above it, supported by an unpeeled redwood log, is an enclosed porch-office. The rustic porch is set off by barn-red board-on-board siding. An interior view of the office (below) conveys its treehouse feel; banks of awning windows open the space to the sights and sounds of the forest.

This porch-turned-office exuberantly demonstrates that walls don't have to impose rigid limits on remodels. The room expands into the rest of the house visually through a fanciful arch, and into the garden literally with a cantilevered bay. Within the bay is the office's focal point—a built-in computer desk that has the well-planned efficiency of a ship's office.

ARCHITECT: TRACEY LOEB/FORMA ARCHITECTS

A SHOPPER'S GUIDE

The home office scene is quickly changing. Rather than recommend particular products, we've tried to sketch current options and identify some basic checkpoints. Armed with this information, you should have little trouble braving today's electronic jungle.

First, shop around. Examine magazine reviews and thumb through mail-order catalogs. Ask friends and business associates to share their experiences. Visit showrooms. Try home-improvement centers and computer superstores, office-supply warehouses and furniture outlets. There are stores that stock nothing but chairs, others that specialize in storage devices. For specific listings, see "Information Sources" on pages 126–127.

It's easy for neophytes in the computerized office to get lost in esoteric terms and concepts. We've tried to keep things simple here. If you don't know software from soft ice cream, don't despair. There's a crash course for digital dummies on page 116.

A striking, U-shaped desk combines polished granite with stainless steel and provides a home for computer, printer, fax, and files—while also furnishing its owner with ample work surfaces.

WORKSTATIONS

If you're coming from the corporate world, you may be accustomed to a big, blocky desk or a modular partition. But at home, your options in workstations are broader—and your choices perhaps a bit narrower.

On the one hand, you can select built-in countertops, task-appropriate computer furnishings, an antique table, or a modular wall system. And, if you like to roam, what about a movable computer cart?

On the negative side, much traditional office furniture is too big for home offices, too sterile, and too expensive. Luckily, furniture designers and manufacturers are getting the message; new designs are aimed not only at the pocketbooks of fledgling entrepreneurs, but also at the scale and decor of their homes.

What's the best setup? It depends on the work you're doing, whether or not you'll be receiving clients or guests, and whether more than one person will be using the office. For starters, review the space-planning principles in "A Planning Primer," pages 9–29.

You expect to "test drive" an office chair before you buy it. Likewise, be sure that a workstation's height, depth, and layout fit you and your work habits.

TRADITIONAL DESKS

An executive desk evokes authority and serves as a focal point for guests and clients. To many of us, that big bulkhead, typically 30 by 60 inches or even larger, still says "serious business." However, these designs evolved for offices, where there's usually plenty of floor space, a file bank next door, and a copier down the hall. Most desks offer limited storage in relation to their footprint. And their 29- or 30-inch height is meant for paperwork, not keyboarding.

On the other hand, if you have the floor space, a desk provides a great opportunity for a design statement—especially if you can combine it with a lower keyboarding surface and storage nearby. A big desktop really allows you to spread things out.

When shopping, you'll find open-, cube-, and closed-style designs in everything from formal walnut and oak to flashy steel and glass. Conference-style desks are designed so that the top overhangs the area where a client would sit. Rolltops and writing desks are other options. A credenza is a traditional desk accessory; it's usually placed behind the desk chair, forming a corridor-like work space.

BUILT-IN COUNTERS

In contrast to most desks, a built-in countertop saves space, follows contours, and can house efficient roll-outs or standing files below. Once installed, it's fixed in place, but you're free to tailor a counter's height and depth to your needs, then customize it with keyboard tray, monitor lift, and other pullouts as you wish (see page 97).

Plastic laminate is the most popular countertop choice and comes in a rainbow of styles, colors, and textures. Laminate is applied over a substrate of ¾-inch particleboard or plywood, and is trimmed

ARCHITECT: GARY EARL PARSONS

An open, L-shaped countertop, surfaced with matte-finish black laminate, bridges his-and-her work areas between flanking maple built-ins. A seamless bullnosed wrapping softens the look of laminate edges.

HERMAN MILLER, INC.

How can you make your office look like home? These two units show the way. Graceful manufactured modules in warm-toned cherry (above) were designed with home environments and budgets in mind. A custom oak desk (right) blends classic Craftsman detailing with clever hinged counters and pullouts.

Sit-stand station

HERMAN MILLER, INC.

INTERIOR DESIGNER: AMOROSO/HOLMAN DESIGN GROUP

to follow the shape—straight, curved, or angled—of the core below. Don't pick a shiny, dark laminate unless you like to clean up dust and fingerprints.

Other options include solid-surface materials, wood, and glass. Solid-surface acrylic, popular for kitchen counters, is pricey, but goes a long way toward turning your office into a home, not the other way around. Wood is a traditional favorite: you can edge-join solid lumber or face hardwood plywood with solid edges and ends.

WORK TABLES

Any table can serve as a work surface, provided it's sturdy and at a comfortable height. We've seen antique farm tables, adjustable drafting tables, kitchen tables, card tables, and striking custom-made tables. If floor space is at a premium, a fold-down table could be just the ticket.

Drafting tables aren't just for draftspersons. The hydraulic type allows you to shift height, angle, and side-to-side position without effort. The counterbalanced table includes a foot rail for people who work standing up.

COMPUTER FURNITURE

The computer has come into its own so quickly that many new users don't quite know what to do with it in their homes.

Solution? You can buy computer stations in any size, from compact carts to elaborate modular suites. Some carts are mobile; others stay put. You can find "sit-stand" adjustable carts, laptop units, and split-height designs. Look for adjustable shelves, wire-management features, and, if you're taking

INTERIOR DESIGNER: SHARON CAMPBELL, ASID

Tables lend an office a casual feel and contribute extra counter space. The custom maple-ply unit at left rolls on locking casters and adjusts from conference height to bench height with a crank of its handle. The waxed pine table shown below brings a warm antique presence to a modern computerized office.

The gray laminate system featured at top on the facing page configures desk, corner, return, peninsula, and hutch modules in a U-shaped layout. The maple-and-metal unit at bottom left has a smaller footprint, combining pullout desk and adjustable shelves in one compact unit. The economical system at far right is built from low-impact strataboard, and is completely adjustable.

INTERIOR DESIGNER: JANET LOHMAN INTERIOR DESIGN

TECHLINE STUDIOS

ARCHITECT: MULDER-KATKOV ARCHITECTURE

NAVIGATOR SYSTEMS

over a living space, doors that close. Knockdown fittings allow you to pack this furniture up and take it with you when you move. Most models require some assembly time, though higher-end dealers may offer shipping and installation services.

Some modular lines resemble wall systems (see below), but they're usually ready-made, not built to order. Typical options include a *desk*; a *return*; a *corner connector* that links desk and return (and often includes a keyboard pullout); a desktop shelf unit or *hutch*; and a *file cabinet*, fixed or mobile. Combining these pieces creates an L-shaped or even U-shaped layout (with a second desk or peninsula). You can begin modestly, then add on—a good bet for someone who's starting a business.

Computer furniture comes in every price range. Typical lower-end units are made from particleboard wrapped with vinyl. Mid-range models may have sturdier melamine or laminate surfaces. The best units

EURODESIGN, LTD.

Modular wall systems have always been flexible; now they've joined the computer age. The system shown at left features cherry veneer and glass, with handy touches such as the printer pullout and articulating keyboard tray. A fold-down work table (top) is a great add-on for a guest-room wall system. The monitor pullout (above) makes use of an awkward corner.

are built from medium-density fiberboard (known as MDF) topped with high-pressure laminate or real wood veneers or from hardwood plywood or strataboard (hardwood chipboard). Some models are, of course, made from solid wood, but these are usually considerably more expensive.

WALL SYSTEMS

Based on modular units that work like building blocks, some wall systems can be put together in hundreds of configurations. A great problem solver, this kind of system produces a high-quality home office virtually out of thin air. It can smoothly meet the special demands of an office that shares space with a bedroom or other living area, or it can squeeze maximum use from a small room.

Wall systems are usually designed to be closed up at the end of the working day. Desks swing down when needed, then up and out of sight when the paperwork is done. Files and equipment slide out for service, then in for storage.

Besides accommodating every peripheral for your computer, from mouse to modem, such a system can even cache a Murphy bed (see page 62), a great idea for guest-room offices. You might also want to extend the system's functions to house electronic entertainment equipment or a family library.

ADD-ONS

Any workstation can be fine-tuned with the ergonomic extras available today. These include articulating keyboard trays (AKTs), slantboards and copy holders, monitor lifts and stands, and custom hardware for pullouts, pop-up printer stands, and swing-up work counters. Several devices are shown at right. For ergonomic guidelines, see pages 18–19.

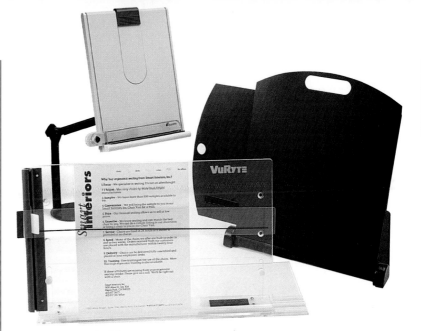

SMART INTERIORS, INC.

Copy holders

Pop-up shelf

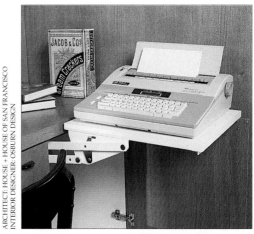

ARCHITECT: HOUSE + HOUSE OF SAN FRANCISCO
INTERIOR DESIGNER: OSBURN DESIGN

Articulating keyboard tray/monitor lift

SMART INTERIORS, INC.

CHAIRS

It may seem surprising, but many experts say that a good chair that fits you well is the single most important purchase to make for your home office. And why not? Studies show that the average office worker spends up to 80 percent of his or her time sitting in that chair. Study after study also shows that productivity falls off drastically when a worker is constantly confined to an ill-fitting chair.

A well-designed chair demonstrates the principles of ergonomics better than any other piece of office furniture. Good desk chairs provide firm support, but at the same time are mobile and instantly adjustable. Look for a chair that moves with you as you shift in it, supporting you both when you lean forward to type or write and when you sink back to talk on the phone.

HERMAN MILLER, INC.

Arm height

Seat height

Tilt tension

Arm angle

Tilt range

Forward tilt

Lumbar height/depth

CHAIR TYPES

Whatever the specific features, office chairs break down into five basic types.

Executive chairs. High-backed office armchairs, also known as executive chairs, tend to be big, roomy, and lush. But before you purchase one of these chairs, be sure that your office can accommodate it.

Don't mistake cushiness for comfort, at least over the long haul. There are plenty of striking, but uncomfortable, executive armchairs out there. An ergonomically sensitive design offers a contoured backrest, instant adjustability, and firmly cushioned support—without sacrificing comfort or luxury.

One notable recent development is the knee-tilt mechanism, shown at right. This pivots an executive chair from the front, not from a weaker center point. What you want is a chair that flexes evenly, without the "listing" motion of older big chairs. Some knee-tilt models can also be locked in a slightly downward position, allowing you to type more comfortably.

You can still find luxurious leather in even the most advanced ergonomic designs. Breathable, slotted-back designs combine air circulation with good support. But leather ups the ante considerably, sometimes doubling a chair's final cost.

Task chairs. Sometimes called "typing" or "secretarial" chairs, task chairs have a lower profile than executive chairs and may or may not have arms (some come either way).

Formerly, typing chairs traded support for mobility. The new task chairs, however, have changed that. A good one adjusts instantly for both height and back flex, allowing you to change your chair's characteristics as your work experience changes.

Look for adjustable arms; good designs adjust both in and out and up and down. Several chair lines offer interchangeable arms. The

JUST CHAIRS

Executive chair

Knee-tilt design

SMART INTERIORS, INC.

Task chair

Shock-absorbing arms

arms should stop short of the chair's front so you can roll right up to a workstation.

Work stools. To work at a drafting table, people sit, stand, or do some combination of the two. For this reason, a high drafting stool usually serves better than a standard desk chair. A good stool should support a person's free and easy movement across the work surface. Some people prefer an adjustable stool; by operating a level under the seat, you can move the chair up or down.

Whether you use a standard stool design or a special model, a footrest is helpful, since your feet may not reach the floor. As with a desk chair, a stool with arms may prove more comfortable. Just be sure they don't interfere with your working motions.

Kneeling chairs. A kneeler has no back. Instead, you sit on a seat that tilts your torso slightly forward and rest your knees on cushions. Even without structural back support, the chair keeps your back straight and free of strain.

Or at least for a while. Many ergonomists and chair retailers are leery of kneeler designs and, citing reports of back and leg pain, dis-

courage their use for principal task seating.

Side chairs. Unless your space is prohibitively small, it's a good idea to provide at least one side chair for a guest or client or, as a change, for yourself. Offices with conference tables will, of course, require extra chairs.

When shopping, you'll find not only a broad selection of shapes, colors, and sizes, but you may discover that even these chairs are more comfortable than in the past.

SHOPPING POINTERS

A good chair requires an investment, it's true, and there's a traditional resistance to spending money on office seating. But an ergonomist might ask why it is that, given the results of health and productivity studies, people who won't bat an eye at a $2,000 computer balk at the idea of a $350 chair.

Chair prices run a gamut from under $100 up to $2,000. But price isn't the only yardstick of quality. The chair must fit you. Mid-range

SMART INTERIORS, INC.

High bench stool

Low stool

JUST CHAIRS

chairs (around $300 to $400) tend to be more flexible and offer better adjustments than cheaper ones. Above that level, you're often paying for material, style, and touches like an upholstered back or bottom.

Find a reputable dealer who will allow you to test a wide variety of chairs and can help fit you to the right one. The best chairs come in several basic sizes. The chair's action must feel tight when you want it tight, and smooth—not loose—when you don't. How positive are the adjustments and where are they located? Can you make them while sitting down, without looking?

Remember that you'll be using your chair for a number of different activities through the course of a

day. Go through the motions of working at a computer, answering the phone, leaning back and staring into space (thinking, of course), writing at a desk or table, or simply rolling across the floor.

The five-star base is now standard, and there are even some six-star designs. These wider bases won't tip like the four-star bases on cheaper chairs.

Carpet casters eliminate the need for ugly, slippery floor mats. If you have a hardwood, vinyl, or masonry floor, look for a different set of "hardwood" casters that are tackier and won't skid.

If you're still uncomfortable, there are several add-ons that can help tailor a chair to your needs. Two popular retrofits are lumbar pads and adjustable footrests.

A built-in window seat makes a cozy counterpoint to the maple desk and wall cases, creating a space-saving alternative to a bulky couch or reading chair.

Side chair

JUST CHAIRS

Adjustable footrest

STORAGE FURNITURE

Chaos can engulf even the most well-conceived and well-equipped home office—that is, unless you have the right storage units and a system to utilize them. If you need some general assistance, see "Get Organized" on pages 22–23. But if it's time to choose specific units, read on. Remember that there's no such thing as having *too much* storage space, so it's best to allow for some future growth now.

FILING SYSTEMS

It's most convenient to store papers such as correspondence, bills, and other written matter in file cabinets. With a carefully organized filing sytem, these papers will be not only securely stored but also readily available when needed.

Standard office files, designed to hold either letter- or legal-size papers, come with drawers arranged either vertically or laterally. *Vertical* files are both more traditional and more readily available. Their depth ranges from 14 to 25 inches; their height depends on the number of drawers in the cabinet.

Lateral files have an average depth of 19 inches and vary in width from 30 to 42 inches. Because of their greater width, they command more wall space than vertical file cabinets. But many people find them easier to use. Stacked in tiers of two or three drawers, lateral file cabinets can double as a room divider. To protect against tipping, make sure that only one drawer can be opened at a time.

HOLD EVERYTHING

Standing files

Open-front files or flip-up files are good for utilizing vertical wall space (you won't have to bend over). The drawback is that you can't use hanging folders for dividers (though specialty products exist).

Or bring the files to you. A roll-around file cabinet can usually hide under a desk or counter when not needed. Some models include a hinged top and a lower file drawer.

Flat files, with their deep, wide drawers, are designed to protect the paper and art boards used by architects, designers, and others. It's important that the drawers glide smoothly, preferably on ball bearings.

Most file cabinets are built from pressed steel. It's worthwhile to spend a little more for sturdy cabinets that glide out easily, won't tip, and have smoothly finished edges (so you won't feel you're going to slash your hand every time you stick it in there). Make sure you have access to the backs of the drawers. Does the unit come with adjustable dividers? Does it include a lock?

Although most metal files suffer from the same drab appearance that afflicts office electronics, you can spray-paint units with custom enamel or epoxy if you choose.

Don't forget wood. In furniture stores and showrooms, you'll find wooden file drawers available as part of modular systems and as separates. Most offerings are veneered (usually in oak), but some are solid.

What about fireproof cabinets? You may find that the models that are *really* rated for fire are prohibitively expensive. One solution: use a small fireproof safe for your most valuable papers and disks, and store other sensitive materials off site.

As these three units show, you needn't be limited by plain, stock file cabinets. The vertical files at top were fashioned from purpleheart and ebony. The flat files at center are jazzed up with color strips and tiny black pulls. At right, a steel unit lends a blast of color to an undercounter space.

INTERIOR DESIGNER: RUTH LIVINGSTON

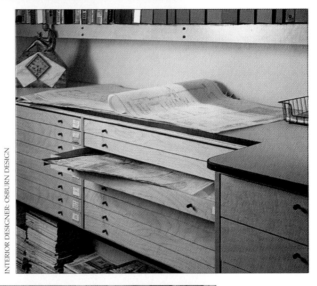

INTERIOR DESIGNER: OSBURN DESIGN

HALLER SYSTEMS

BOOKSHELVES

Whether stacked to the ceiling in a dozen horizontal layers or aligned as an inconspicuous pair, shelves are a useful addition to almost every office. Though most often filled with books, periodicals, and the like, shelves also make handy repositories for office supplies, plants, even knickknacks.

Inexpensive and easy to install, wall-mounted shelving has two other advantages: it's flexible—allowing you to place any number of shelves where you need them—and it has a lighter appearance than other shelving styles.

The *track-and-bracket* style (see facing page) allows you to tailor a complex shelving system to fit your specific needs. The tracks need to be screwed into wall studs to support the weight of the shelves and the items stored on them.

Large, decorative *brackets* and *gussets* are more attractive but less flexible. Here, you screw the brackets themselves to the studs.

Most industrial shelving is made of metal. Bookcases are available in unfinished wood, wood veneer, brightly enameled metal, and other high-tech dressings. Of course, you can also have shelves custom-designed and built by a cabinetmaker to fit under windows, over doors, inside closets, and into oddly shaped spaces.

Built-in cases have a clean, smoothly integrated appearance that sometimes intrudes less upon an office layout and design style than

Shelving units tame office chaos. Shown clockwise from top left: a hanging rack for magazines and a bookcase on wheels (just give it a pull); a deskside ladder of oak and acrylic; a set of magazine-size display cubbies; and a brash yellow wire-rack system.

INTERIOR DESIGNER: BAUER INTERIOR DESIGN

INTERIOR DESIGNER: OSBURN DESIGN

INTERIOR DESIGNER: VAN-MARTIN ROWE INTERIOR DESIGN STUDIO

INTERIOR DESIGNER: SHARON CAMPBELL, ASID

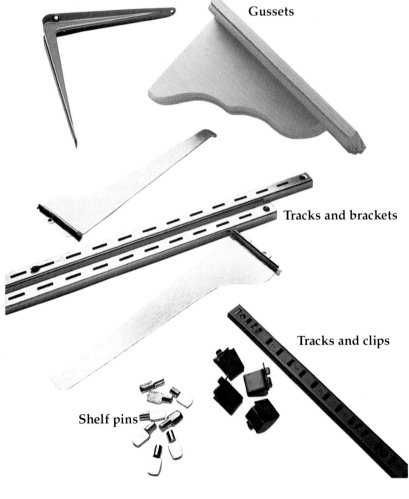

Gussets

Tracks and brackets

Tracks and clips

Shelf pins

Recessed glass-doored library cases, crafted in hardwood with brass accents, form a classic backdrop for a formal, wood-paneled study.

ARCHITECT: REMICK ASSOCIATES ARCHITECTS-BUILDERS, INC.

ARCHITECT: SANBORN DESIGNS INCORPORATED

An eclectic storage style mixes built-in bookcases, wooden flat files, and an artist's collection of containers. Woven baskets store paper samples; wooden boxes and ceramic ware corral pens and brushes.

other shelving options. Mounting the shelves on *tracks and clips* (see page 105) or with adjustable pins lets you arrange them in exactly the configuration you need. In earthquake country, plan to anchor either the back or the side of the case to wall framing.

Be sure not to overload your shelves. Maximum spans between supports are 24 inches for particleboard, 30 inches for ¾-inch pine, 36 inches for ¾-inch plywood, and 48 inches for ¾- or 1-inch hardwood. Thicker shelves allow longer spans.

SUPPLY CONTAINERS

Suitable storage for office supplies depends on the nature of your business, the size of your office, and the amount of supplies you need to store. Beyond this, the choice of containers depends solely on your personal taste.

Some home offices, such as those occupying an outgrown child's room, come equipped with built-in supply storage in the form of roomy closets. Sometimes a cabinet can be built into a wall. You can also purchase many types and styles of storage furniture, from contemporary designs to antique cabinets. You'll see numerous examples throughout this book.

Kitchen cabinets are too high to serve as work surfaces, but they're fine for standing tasks and for supporting office machines. You'll find stock, custom, and custom-modular units in cabinet showrooms. Pantry packs and other tall freestanding cabinets can really hold a lot. And don't overlook closet systems.

For desktop storage, you'll find plenty of choices at any office store or closet store. Several are shown at upper right. This is a place to let your creativity shine. For some initial ideas, see the box at right.

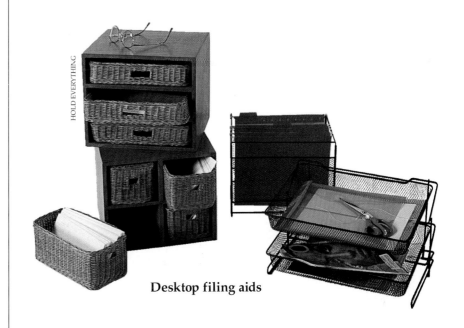

HOLD EVERYTHING

Desktop filing aids

STORAGE OPTIONS

When it comes to storage, you have a lot of choices. Do you prefer fixed or movable units, or some combination? Would traditional desk drawers be adequate, or do you want a more fluid combination? What about wall shelving or cabinets?

Here's a quick checklist of storables and storage alternatives you may wish to consider.

■ Pencils and office supplies: molded cutlery insert for standard kitchen drawer; desktop bins; carpenter's tool caddy with handle; add-on drawer pullout; supply cabinet or armoire

■ Files and tear sheets: vertical files; flat files; roll-around cart; open-front cabinets; milk crates; desktop dividers; cardboard file boxes (for out-of-room storage)

■ Books and magazines: freestanding bookcase; open shelves or wall case with dividers; built-in wall rack; acrylic dividers; binders; stackable bins

■ Electronics: modular computer cart; pullout shelves and drawers; audio-visual cart or specialized mounting hardware; "appliance garage" or desktop cabinets with flipper or tambour doors; armoire; ventilated closet or kitchen pantry pack

LIGHTING

Designers divide lighting into three categories: task, ambient, and accent. Task lighting illuminates a particular area where a visual activity—such as drawing, reading, or bill paying—takes place. Ambient, or general, lighting fills the undefined areas of a room with a soft level of light—enough, say, to shuffle between file cabinet and fax machine. Accent, or mood, lighting is used to highlight architectural features or display objects, to set a style, or to provide drama.

One of several lighting plans might meet your office needs; the fixtures should also fit in with your design scheme. But before fixture shopping, take a tip from lighting pros: consider the source, or the bulb, first.

BULBS & TUBES

Light sources can be grouped according to the way they produce light. A collection of representative bulbs is shown below at left.

Incandescent light. This light, the kind used most frequently in our homes, is produced by a tungsten thread that burns slowly inside a glass bulb. "A" bulbs are the old standbys; "R" and "PAR" bulbs produce a more controlled beam; and silvered-bowl types diffuse light and cut glare. A number of decorative bulbs are also available.

Low-voltage incandescent lighting is especially useful for accent lighting. Operating on 12 or 24 volts, these lights require transformers (often built into the fixtures) to step down the voltage from standard 120-volt household circuits.

Fluorescent light. Fluorescent tubes are unrivaled for energy efficiency. They also last far longer than incandescent bulbs.

In the past, fluorescent tubes have been criticized for noise, flicker, and poor color rendition. Electronic ballasts and better fixture shielding have remedied the first two problems; as for the last one, manufacturers have developed fluorescents in a

Here's a sampling of light sources and switches. Shown clockwise from upper left: fluorescent options, including U-shaped and globe retrofits for standard fixtures; frosted, clear, and nonglare incandescent bulbs; MR-16 and other halogen sources; and new dimmer designs.

wide spectrum of colors, from warm (about 2,700° Kelvin) to very cool (about 6,300° Kelvin).

These days, it's much simpler to blend fluorescent with tungsten or halogen sources than in the past. And you're no longer limited to big, clunky tubes. Compact fluorescent bulbs fit downlights and other small fixtures and can be retrofitted to standard incandescent lamps with the use of an adapter.

Quartz halogen. These bright, white newcomers are excellent for task lighting, accenting, and other dramatic effects. Halogen is often low-voltage but may use standard line current. The popular MR-16 bulb creates the tightest beam; for a longer reach and wider coverage, choose a PAR bulb. There's an abundance of smaller bulb shapes and sizes to fit task lamps, pendants, and undercabinet strip lights.

LIGHT LEVELS

How much lighting do you need? As a rule of thumb, in an average room the most visually demanding tasks require a total of at least 2,500 lumens. (Lumens and wattage are listed on a bulb's sleeve.) Part of the total should be ambient light, but the greatest number of lumens should be concentrated in task lighting. An older worker may need twice the light that a 20-year-old needs.

But it's the ratio between task lighting and background that induces eyestrain and fatigue. According to one study, there should be no more than about a 3-to-1 ratio between computer screen and immediate work area; and no more than a 10-to-1 divergence from other bright or dark room areas.

How can you tell what's what? If you own a 35mm SLR camera or a good light meter, the 3-to-1 ratio equals a difference between readings of 1½ f-stops; a 10-to-1 spread equals 3½ stops.

COMPARING LIGHT BULBS & TUBES

INCANDESCENT

A-bulb
Description. Familiar pear shape; frosted or clear.
Uses. Everyday household use.

T—Tubular
Description. Tube-shaped, from 5" long. Frosted or clear.
Uses. Appliances, cabinets, decorative fixtures.

R—Reflector
Description. White or silvered coating directs light out end of funnel-shaped bulb.
Uses. In directional fixtures; focuses light where needed.

PAR—Parabolic aluminized reflector
Description. Similar to auto headlamp; special shape and coating project light and control beam.
Uses. In recessed downlights and track fixtures.

Silvered bowl
Description. A-bulb, with silvered cap to cut glare and produce indirect light.
Uses. In track fixtures and pendants.

Low-voltage strip lights
Description. Like Christmas tree lights; in strips or tracks, or encased in flexible, waterproof plastic.
Uses. Task lighting and decoration.

FLUORESCENT

Tube
Description. Tube-shaped, 5" to 96" long. Needs special fixture and ballast.
Uses. Shadowless work light; also indirect lighting.

PL—Compact tube
Description. U-shaped with base; 5¼" to 7½" long.
Uses. In recessed downlights; some PL tubes include ballasts to replace A-bulbs.

QUARTZ HALOGEN

High-intensity
Description. Small, clear bulb with consistently high light output; used in halogen fixtures.
Uses. In specialized task lamps, torchères, and pendants.

Low-voltage MR-16 (mini-reflector)
Description. Tiny (2"-diameter) projector bulb; gives small circle of light from a distance.
Uses. In low-voltage track fixtures, mono-spots, and recessed downlights.

Low-voltage PAR
Description. Similar to auto headlamp, tiny filament, shape, and coating give precise direction.
Uses. To project a small spot of light a long distance.

ARCHITECT: HOUSE + HOUSE OF SAN FRANCISCO. INTERIOR DESIGNER: OSBURN DESIGN

Small and discreet or big and brash—office lighting options run the gamut. Trim track fixtures (near right) move along tracks and pivot, providing accurate aim; recessed downlights (far right) may be fitted with a variety of bulbs and baffles. Task lamps (below) are instantly adjustable and come in a wide range of halogen, incandescent, and fluorescent models.

MOSS LIGHTING

WHICH FIXTURES?

For home offices, you can choose among adjustable, surface-mounted, recessed, and movable fixtures. The key is combining them into an effective, flexible lighting scheme. And remember that glare can be a big problem around workstations; see page 25 for guidelines.

Task lamps. Using an adjustable desk lamp is often the best way to direct bright task light where you want it. A task lamp is a personal choice; inquire about a try-out period at home before you buy. Halogen lamps produce the cleanest, brightest beam, while PL fluorescent models are tops for reducing glare and shadows.

But consider other task-lighting options, too. One popular method, borrowed from kitchen design, is to mount fluorescent tubes or incandescent or halogen strip lights below overhanging wall cabinets or shelves; the bulbs are baffled from view with wood or metal trim.

Downlights or tracks, typically used for ambient or accent needs, can highlight a floating desk or follow a built-in counter. When augmented with one or more task lamps, they can greatly reduce shadows.

Ambient lighting. Remember that ambient lighting simply helps you get from place to place and fills in the shadows left by task lighting. You won't need a lot. Recessed downlights, track fixtures, and surface-mounted pendants are all common choices. For shadow control, it's best to have more than one source.

Accents. Portable uplights, wall washers, torchères, neon strips, and hidden soffit tubes all add decorative accents and, if dimmer-controlled, also serve as ambient sources.

Both low-voltage tracks and downlights can be fitted with shields or baffles that produce a wide range of effects.

TAME THOSE WIRES

It's a silent epidemic. Forget the paper-free revolution: how about a cord-free revolution? Between task lamps, computer, printer, modem, fax machine, and a swarm of phone lines, wires can create a real Gordian knot above and below your desk.

Fortunately, a new generation of wire-management devices, several of which are pictured below, now comes to the rescue.

Desktop *grommets*, round or oblong and available in numerous sizes and finishes, are probably the easiest aids to find. To install one, drill through the desktop with a hole-saw attachment (it looks like a big cookie cutter). Tape the surface to prevent it from chipping. Tap the grommet into the hole, feed wires through, then push or pivot the cap into place.

Troughs direct cords along the back of a desk to a point where they can all exit. *Vertical channels* direct wires to the floor and match some troughs. *Friction clips* hold wires tight to the desk like brooms in a broom closet. *Raceways* mount to desk, wall, or floor and direct wires anywhere. *Surge protectors* (see page 119) not only guard against power spikes but help consolidate your plugs and wires, too.

Low-tech solutions include electrical wire ties, hook-and-loop straps stuck to desk bottom or back, and electrical-cable or phone-wire staples. For long runs, try feeding a mess of wires below the floor or through an adjacent wall inside PVC conduit.

Grommets, raceways, and troughs are showing up at some office-supply, computer, and hardware stores; otherwise, try office or woodworking mail-order sources (for listings, see page 126). You'll find wire ties, plastic conduit, and other handy devices at electrical supply houses and in the electrical departments of some home-improvement centers and hardware stores.

COMPUTERS

More and more home offices center around a personal computer. A most versatile office assistant, it handles a wide variety of tasks, from word processing to record-keeping to financial planning to database functions. Hooked to a phone line via a modem or fax modem (pages 124–125), your computer allows you to exchange information with other computers throughout the world.

Before you invest in a particular machine, however, you'll want to learn about the latest technological developments. Our descriptions and outlines of basic options are meant to help you comparison shop for a computer and plan an office space to accommodate it.

When shopping, you'll encounter a dense thicket of jargon: terms like RAM, byte, DOS, and WYSIWYG abound. Need a translation? See page 116 for help.

DESKTOP COMPUTERS

Rule number one: there's always a newer and better machine, one that's also the most expensive thing around. The question is, do you need it? The best buys are at the next level down—and in computer time, that means about six months to a year.

IBM-compatible or Mac? The most basic decision is between an IBM-compatible machine—also called a PC, a clone, or a DOS or Windows machine (after the operating systems that run them)—and an Apple Macintosh. Although this great divide is narrowing, and trans-

lating packages allow you to run some of one system's programs on the other, it's still not a perfect union.

PCs are known for their number-crunching abilities, their adaptability, and their universality. They're usually the preferred business machine, and the great majority of business software is written for PCs. They're also generally less expensive.

On the other hand, the Macintosh is the machine preferred by most designers, graphic artists,

Compact disks

Floppy disks

IBM-compatible 486 computer

Apple Power Macintosh computer

desktop publishers, and others who communicate primarily in visual terms rather than with numbers. Macs are known for their easy-to-use menu interface and WYSIWYG (what-you-see-is-what-you-get) screen displays; and even though Windows has improved DOS machines, it's still much easier for a beginner to use a Mac.

Often the choice boils down to the machine that can communicate best with those of the customers and clients you're working with.

PC or Mac, there are several checkpoints around which computer discussions and comparisons revolve. Here's a rundown.

The CPU. This internal engine, or central processing unit, is what drives the computer. Talk about CPUs usually veers toward the nature of the microprocessor chips that run them, and to their operating speeds.

In the turbulent DOS world, so-called 286 and 386 chips are dinosaurs, an 80486 or 486 is standard, and the Pentium (586) is currently king of the hill. The numbers keep going up. Certain tags like

486SX or 486DXII indicate speedier variations on the basic chip. Though the Pentium is top dog, it commands a premium price and requires special software to take full advantage of its lightning speed. Unless your business involves heavy, continuous number crunching, most office consultants recommend a 486 machine that's upgradable later.

Top-of-the-line Macs now feature the Power PC microprocessor; but again, you'll need to acquire custom software to maximize its benefits. Unless you require cutting-edge graphics capabilities, the best buys are in the "family" line (currently the Performa machines), featuring a fast 68040 processor that's also upgradable.

After chip type, the next checkpoint is clock speed, measured in megahertz (MHz). Higher numbers indicate greater speed. For general office use, shop for a minimum of 25 or 33 MHz; for heavy work with numbers or graphics, 50 or 66 MHz is preferred.

A math coprocessor helps speed the handling of complex spread-

sheets. But if you'll be working primarily with word-processing or check-writing software, don't bother.

The memory. RAM (or random access memory) dictates how much information your computer can handle at once. Today's operating systems and software packages gobble RAM at rates unheard of five years ago. Fortunately, memory is getting both cheaper and more compact. Consider 4 megabytes (MB) of RAM the bare minimum; 8 to 12 MB is now standard.

Disk drives. Your computer's disk drive stores the huge backlog of information that is shuttled in and out of RAM as required. Given the insatiable appetites of today's software, operating systems, and assorted bells and whistles, the recommended disk-drive capacity keeps climbing up and up. Most experts now quote 200 MB as the bottom line for a general business machine, though a writer, for example, might need far less. Like filing drawers, closet space, or life in general, you may find there's never too much or too many, so it pays to plan ahead.

Ports and slots. Be sure you have enough serial ports in the back of the computer to accommodate add-ons you may want, such as an external modem, monitor, mouse, or scanner. And be sure a new computer has at least three or four open expansion slots. These allow you to upgrade and add goodies like video memory, a fax modem, or voice mail without having to start over.

What about multimedia? The latest buzzword in computer stores is "multimedia," fueled by the CD-ROM drive and its 680 MB capacity. Sound, graphics, animation, and real-time video are the attractions, and they all run at once. You can get a whole encyclopedia on one disk.

Fun and informative, yes, but does your office need one? Remember that ROM stands for "read-only memory"—you can't store new information on a CD, you can only play what's there. Still, it seems inevitable that more and more reference information and software packaging will go this route, and that the floppy disk will go the way

of the dodo and Edsel. CD-ROM drives are now relatively slow, but getting faster.

The big picture. Monitors come in sizes from 13- and 14-inch "standards" up to 20- and 21-inch monsters (size is measured on the diagonal). Once you hit the 15- to 16-inch zone, prices begin to jump, and you may need an add-on video card to drive the display.

Most people prefer color, but do you really need it? Though prices are dropping steeply, a color screen might still cost double what a comparable gray-scale model does. You'll see terms like 8-bit (256 colors), 16-bit (thousands), and 24-bit (literally millions), indicating numbers of colors available. The bigger your screen and the more bits you want, the more video memory you'll need.

Resolution in the PC world means VGA (video graphics array) or, preferably, Super VGA. For Mac screens, a resolution of 1,024 x 768 pixels is considered good. Also look for a dot pitch (the diagonal spacing

between screen dots) of .28 mm or smaller (the smaller the number, the higher the resolution). In general, the flatter a screen is, the less it distorts.

The monitor should be bright (25 footlamberts or more), be easily adjustable for angle and tilt, and have easy-to-work controls on the front so you can see the effects of your adjustments.

Look for one of two Swedish emission certifications—either MPRII or the newer, stricter TCO standard.

A slow refresh rate (the speed at which the screen redraws an image) can cause eyestrain and headaches. For most viewers, a 60 Hz refresh rate is considered good; if you're particularly sensitive, look for a 70 to 75 Hz rating.

Keyboards. Unless you're ready to abandon the classic QWERTY arrangement, keyboard selection is

Ergonomic keyboard

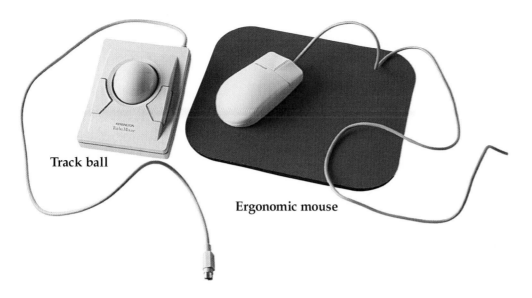

Track ball

Ergonomic mouse

largely a matter of touch. Choose a key action that allows you to push down with only moderate pressure and that has an audible and tactile click you're comfortable with. Some keyboards have adjustable action.

Programmable keys are a boon: not only can you customize the placement of function keys, but you can set up macros (multistep operations), allowing you to cut keyboarding time.

A slimmer, trimmer keyboard profile allows you to achieve the correct wrist angle more easily (see pages 18–19). Some keyboards are adjustable; wrist rests (shown at right) and improvised shims can also help.

You'll also find a growing number of ergonomically designed keyboards. Most split or bend the keyboard (as shown on the facing page) to help minimize ulnar deviation (splayed hands). But "ergonomic" is an imprecise term; the key is to find what works for you.

Mouse or manpower? The mouse, once a Mac-only goody, has now entered the PC world, too. A mouse in hand helps you scurry with one motion from spot to spot—instead of tootling around the screen with the arrow keys on your keyboard.

But mouse use, by its relentless nature, is suspected as a cause of some repetitive wrist and hand injuries. In response, new ergonomic designs are hitting the market. Track balls, which look like upside-down mice (the base stays put), are loved by some, cursed by others. Though there's no proof, some ergonomic experts feel they reduce the risk of some injuries.

The graphically inclined might prefer a pen- or stylus-based digital tablet, others a joystick. And there are bound to be new input devices waiting in the wings.

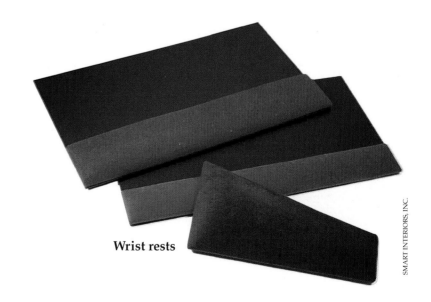

Wrist rests

SMART INTERIORS, INC.

A DIGITAL DICTIONARY

Never has such a mudslide of jargon rolled onto the office scene as accompanied the rise of the personal computer. This logjam of acronyms, buzzwords, slang, and codes can seem like a foreign tongue to the uninitiated. And though most terms are benign, the learning curve presents a major hurdle to some attempting to join the digital age—one even greater than actually running the computer.

The typical personal computer consists of a microprocessor housed in a central processing unit or CPU, a floppy and/or hard disk drive, a monitor (like a TV screen), a keyboard, and a printer (like a cross between copier and typewriter). These parts are called "hardware"; the computer runs "software" that allows you to type a letter, make a contact file, or pay your taxes.

When you're shopping or asking advice, you're sure to run into all of these terms and, with the rapid rate of development within the field, probably several more. But here's a cheat sheet.

Byte. A basic unit of computer memory. Also megabyte or MB (1,000 bytes) and gigabyte (1,000,000 bytes or 1,000 megabytes)—about the current limit of hard disks.

CD-ROM. The disk looks just like a rock 'n' roll CD, but stores up to 680 K of multimedia text, graphics, and/or sound that plays on your computer. ROM stands for "read-only memory." You can't add information to a CD—at least, not yet.

Chip. A micro-sized circuit etched onto a tiny silicon backing board, providing the myriad electrical pathways that power a PC's microprocessor.

CPU, or central processing unit. The brains behind your computer, including chips, microprocessor, fan, and other mysterious goblins.

Cyberspace. Electronic space bridged by computers and technology. Virtual corporations and virtual communities operate in cyberspace—i.e., over phone lines.

Digital. As opposed to analog, meaning a device has been encoded numerically rather than by mechanical means. And those are binary numbers, pardner.

Disk drive. This mobilizes memory that's moved in and out of RAM as required, then saved as data files. Drives can be either hard or floppy (see below).

DOS, or disk operating system, as in MS-DOS. The language that runs IBM-compatible computers. Windows is a menu-driven version of DOS.

E-mail, or electronic mail. As opposed to "snail mail," the overland version. Simply means a message transported by computer instead of by the post office. E-mail can come via a local network, an online service, or the Internet.

Floppy disk. The original 5¼-inch disks looked like old 45 rpm records; they're fading from use. Later 3½-inch disks held about 800 K; high-density disks hold about 1.4 MB. Yes, the originals were sort of floppy, but the rigid 3½-inch versions are not.

Font. A typeface, either an on-screen font or a printer font. If your computer is WYSIWYG (see below), the two should match. Boldface and italic versions of one type family are considered separate fonts.

Hard disk. A high-volume storage tank (typically 200 MB) for both software files and your collection of data. There are both external and internal hard disks, but most are internal.

Hardware. Just as a hammer is a piece of hardware, the physical computer parts—computer chassis, disk drive, etc.—are also called hardware. For a comparison, see Software, below.

Information highway. A politicized metaphor for the coming digital age. It's not just a highway for computers but also for other interconnected digital media—phones, cable TV, and information services. Unlike some other on line developments, the information highway is mostly a field for big commercial players.

Menu, as in pull-down menu. Allows you to point and click on a printed or graphic command rather than having to type in esoteric keyboard codes. This is Apple's claim to fame, now emulated by Windows for DOS -based machines.

Multimedia. Simply any assemblage of text, image, and sound played out by your computer's screen and speakers. "Interactive" is a related term: it means that you can respond to what's going on, directing the flow of multimedia information wherever you choose.

Multitasking. Another buzzword that simply means the ability to work with more than one on-screen application at once. A trademark feature of multimedia presentations and of splashy new operating systems.

Network. A hookup between two or more computers allowing them to share software, hard disk space, and data. Most are cable-connected, but you can also buy remote network devices. Multicomputer home offices often use local area networks (LANs).

Operating system. As in DOS, Windows, OS-2, Unix, Macintosh System 7. The mediating link between your desktop, your software, and your microprocessor.

Peripheral. An overly elaborate term for any accessory or add-on to your basic computer—e.g., a printer or modem.

RAM, or random access memory. The pool of information from which you can draw at any one time on-screen. Or, to invoke an often used metaphor, it's similar to how many open file folders you could cram onto the top of a desk.

Software. As opposed to hardware (above). An application or "program" that focuses a PC's power on your particular task. Most programs come on one or more floppy disks.

Telecommuting. Home-based work for an office employee; telecommunications hardware and software link the worker remotely with a company's PC network or mainframe system. For details, see pages 122–123.

WYSIWYG. An acronym for "what you see is what you get," meaning that the printed page should look like the screen display. That's important when running desktop publishing, drawing, or graphics programs.

LAPTOPS TO PALMTOPS

If you're dreaming of a mobile office, you'll certainly want to look at the latest portable computers. Sizes range, in descending order, from laptop to notebook to subnotebook to palmtop (or handbook).

Portables are constantly dropping in size and weight while bulking up in RAM and disk capacity. Early laptops weighed about 20 pounds (they looked and felt like sewing machines), but current notebooks run from 3½ to 7 pounds. Most fit inside a briefcase. They run on either battery power or AC power, using an adapter.

Could you use a notebook model as your sole office computer? Yes, and many people do. But try out the keyboard. Is it too cramped for continuous use? Are the keys in familiar places, or rearranged in an annoying way? Ask about battery life and battery-saving features. Ask about fax modem add-ons (see pages 124–125) and PCMCIA expansion slots.

Do you need color? You'll pay more, and you'll go through batteries faster. Gray-scale displays come in passive- and active-matrix versions; active-matrix is tops, but still pricey. Check screen brightness and backlighting. How well can you see from an angle? How well could you see in a dim cafe?

The docking computer aims to bridge the desktop-notebook gap. On the road, it's a notebook; at home, it slides into a housing with hot-wire contacts and can be used as the CPU with a larger monitor and keyboard.

Then there are palmtops, pocket organizers, and PDAs (personal digital assistants). These devices can house your contact lists, calendar, and daily notes. Think of a PDA as a mobile link to your home computer; some are downloadable and have fax capabilities.

Subnotebook computer

Notebook computer

Docking computer

Personal digital assistant

PRINTERS

A printer is the typewriter of the computer age; in fact, the few typewriters we've seen recently are used mostly for envelopes (still a printer's weak spot).

There are three main printer types: dot matrix, ink jet, and laser. The one you need depends on the work you do, your presentation needs, and your budget.

Dot matrix. Unlike the early daisy wheel, the dot matrix still survives, but is becoming a dinosaur due to ink jet prices (see below). That familiar whining, screeching noise is the result of metal pins hammering tiny dots through a ribbon onto the paper, either single sheets or continuous-feed bundles. If you can stand the noise and are mostly processing duplicate forms, spreadsheet figures, or payroll checks, then a dot matrix machine may do the trick—especially since you can buy used ones for practically nothing.

Ink jets. These are the newcomers, and unless you need a laser printer's special features, adequate for most office needs. Images are formed by tiny dots actually squirted onto the paper, so they're crisper and much quieter than dot matrix models.

Resolution is the same as that of laser printers of just a couple years ago, and ink jets are much less expensive. Another plus: models with vertical paper feeds have a smaller footprint than other printers. Ink jets also take to color beautifully. But be advised: the cost of ink cartridges makes these machines more expensive to operate than laser printers, and most ink jet printers run at only half the speed.

Laser printers. These are still tops, making cleaner type and better graphics than ink jets. Standard resolution is 300 dots per inch (dpi), but some lasers now produce 600 dpi.

Printer speed ranges from 4 pages per minute (ppm) to about 10 ppm; trimmer, less expensive models are generally slower. Any new laser printer will probably have 1 MB of built-in memory, but 2 MB is better, and for complex graphics you'll want 4 MB or more.

You'll pay considerably more for a machine with PostScript capability. If you're producing text only, you probably won't need PostScript; but some drawing, design, and desktop publishing programs require it.

When evaluating a laser printer, ask about maintenance. How well does it print envelopes or labels? Can you add a fax feature? How many fonts are included? Laser fonts come in both expansion-card form (for DOS machines) and soft, or downloadable, form (for Macs).

Portables. Five years ago, who would have thought you could tuck a printer into a shoulder bag right alongside your notebook computer?

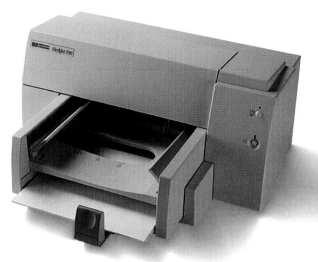

Ink jet printer

Laser printer

These new portables, as svelte as 3 pounds or less, are mostly scaled-down ink jet machines without the feed trays. Like notebook computers, they run either on batteries or by AC adapter.

SCANNERS

Want to import drawings, text, or graphics from the real world into your computer programs? Then the scanner's your tool.

The flatbed scanner is the standard; it looks and works much like a desktop copier (see page 125), only it converts a document to digital form and sends it to your computer. Hand-held scanners are much cheaper, but typically scan only 4 inches at a time. The sheetfed scanner has the price advantage and informality of the hand-held, but accepts documents from business cards up to full 8½- by 11-inch sheets.

Scanners come in black-and-white, gray-scale, and color versions. Black-and-white is fine for rough recording, but you'll need gray-scale for photos and graphics. Color hogs a huge amount of disk space, so plan to skip this unless you're a graphics pro.

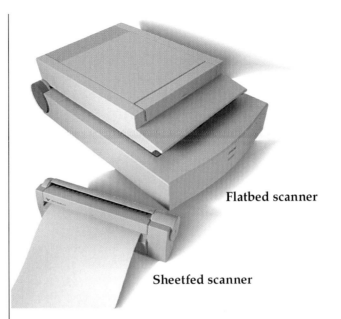

Flatbed scanner

Sheetfed scanner

Portable printer

BACKUP DEVICES

As more of us are entrusting our business and personal records to the computer, the shadow of a potential glitch or crash grows longer. Make it a point to protect and back up your work frequently; the devices below can help.

Surge protectors. A surge protector shields against the sudden surges of power, called "spikes," that occasionally enter house wiring or occur when a refrigerator or other large appliance switches off. Such jolts can damage a computer's memory.

Most surge protectors look like a standard power strip and have a built-in on/off switch and a circuit breaker. Another type has a master socket, allowing you to turn on an assemblage of machines (a printer, scanner, and modem, for example) by switching on just one of them.

UPSs. An uninterruptible power supply or UPS keeps you up and running long enough in a brownout or blackout to save your files, quit your program, and turn off your computer. Look for the "standby"

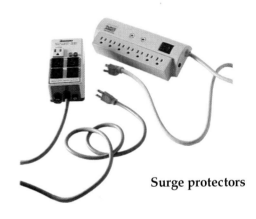

Surge protectors

type—one with a battery that only kicks into gear as needed. It's cheaper and quieter than so-called "continuous" designs.

Tape backups, cartridge backups. And what if you collect more data than you can physically back up on a regular basis? Enter the data cartridge tape or tape backup.

A tape backup is also handy for clearing huge graphic, video, or multimedia files off your hard drive. But it's not a good playback device (it's linear, like an audio tape). If you do a lot of such memory-intensive work, you might consider the pricier removable cartridge drive—commonly known as a Bernoulli (DOS) or Syquist (Mac) drive.

COMMUNICATIONS

Besides the personal computer, communications technology is another crucial segment of the trail leading workers home.

Phone, modem, and fax can keep you in touch with the outside world—instantly. And it doesn't matter whether you're down the hall or a thousand miles away. Want to expand your business into cyberspace? See "Going Online?" on pages 122–123.

PHONE OPTIONS

You'll find conventional phones in all shapes and sizes, from simple one-line desk phones to two-line phones featuring single-button memory dialing, auto redialing, built-in speaker, mute button, and distinctive ringing. In addition, your phone company can provide a stack of add-on services for a small fee; for a sampling, see the box on page 124.

But the real news in phones is all the other options you now have. If portability, mobility, and programmability are key features to you, take a look at the following products.

Cordless phones. Undeniably handy for the home office, a portable phone not only frees you from cords, but allows you to conduct business from the kitchen, the mailbox, or the garden. It's also a real boon for those with stay-at-home kids.

The newer phones come with the same features as desk phones—such as built-in speaker, program-

Headset

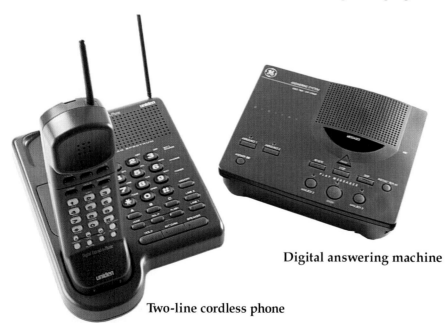

Two-line cordless phone

Digital answering machine

mable dialing, auto redial, and a mute button (you can hear your caller, but your caller can't hear your five-year-old screaming in the background).

For best transmission, look for new 900 MHz digital technology. Also ask about batteries; some new ones last for up to three weeks. Is the phone able to recharge on its base, or will it inevitably run down while sitting?

Portables won't work if the power's out, so you may want an office backup.

Mobile headsets. We saw a lot of these on our travels, and with good reason: if you do a lot of phone duty, a lightweight headset not only frees your hands, but sidesteps the discomfort of crimping a traditional handset between neck and shoulder. Although you could use a speaker phone while working, its hollow sound is a turnoff to many callers.

You'll find both hard-wired and remote headsets, with or without dialing pads. A remote headset is cordless; you simply clip a lightweight receiver to your belt.

Cellular phones. Seen as techno toys until just recently, cellular phones are now considered standard equipment in the "floating" or mobile office picture.

So-called car phones were the originals. They're hard-wired to a mount on dashboard or floor and require a remote antenna.

Transportable or "bag" phones pack a handset, dialing pad, antenna, and rechargeable battery within a self-contained case. Though portable, they're heavy—about 5 pounds.

Flip or portable phones are the ultimate in cellular mobility. You can fold them up and stick them in a handbag or glove compartment, then flick them into talk mode à la James Bond or Dick Tracy. Some batteries allow up to 12 hours in standby mode; otherwise you can run them off a car's cigarette lighter.

So why buy anything but a flip phone? As usual, there's one hitch, and it's power. In most urban areas, the flip phone's 0.6-watt output is considered adequate; but in hilly or remote areas, it can't match the performance of 3-watt transportables or car phones. You can buy so-called car kits for your flip phone that boost power when driving, but they're likely to be expensive.

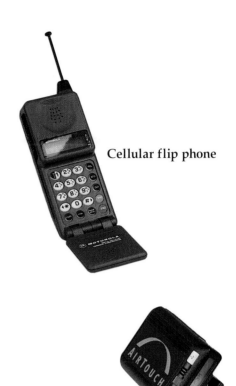

Cellular flip phone

Pager

Pagers. Why get a beeper? To some, it's the last link that lets them stay in touch while working or playing anywhere, anytime. (That's a good thing to some, a curse to others.) Pagers are also less expensive and less intrusive than cellular phones—especially if you get a model that vibrates or flashes instead of beeping.

Some pagers have multiple-number memories; others store short messages entered by the paging service. You can explore a variety of service agreements—local, regional, and national.

Answering machines. The now-ubiquitous answering machine is also undergoing continuing developments, while experiencing a serious challenge from both voice-mail services and voice-mail computer cards (see page 124).

All-digital machines are currently tops; they're smaller and more hassle-free than traditional tape

(Continued on page 124)

Cellular bag phone

GOING ONLINE?

Every week millions of people, many of them home-based workers, pick up the phone and dial into electronic cyberspace. Telecommuters check in with their main offices. Travelers link their notebook computers to home units many miles away. Professionals complete their market research, business banking, trip reservations, and correspondence via computer screen. Virtual corporations, whose partners have never stood face to face, go about their daily business.

Sound farfetched? It's happening everywhere. And the hardware you need to do it yourself is surprisingly simple: a personal computer, a telephone line, a modem, some telecommunications software, and the phone number of another modem that's hooked up to a second computer, an online service, or the Internet.

Here's a brief description of some basic business options that allow you to do your commuting over phone lines.

Telecommuting Tips

Generally speaking, telecommuting is work that's done by an employee at home, rather than at the employer's office. It doesn't have to be a computer-based task, but the computer's networking abilities have helped open the door to telecommuting at large.

Technologically, if your work is computer-based and you can duplicate—or "emulate"—your office workstation elsewhere, then you can do it from a home office. A modem links your home to the corporate base, allowing you to access relevant data files from an office network, file work reports, or simply pass E-mail messages back and forth. Fax, copier, phone, and overnight mail help fill in the cracks.

Due to tough new state commuting laws and corporate downsizing, many companies are taking a fresh look at telecommuting, and some are happy to provide either office equipment or an equipment allowance to satellite employees.

The toughest nut to crack seems to be the human element. Traditional office environments were built around direct supervision, and it's hard for some managers—and some employees—to feel comfortable otherwise. Telecommuting consultants recommend that you begin slowly, then map out a detailed plan with your supervisor—one based on tangible goals that you can both check off as accomplished.

Telecommuters report the same problems as others who first move home: isolation, family distractions, and lack of self-discipline. Some miss the office social structure; others feel out of the loop and worry about being passed over for promotions or special assignments. Some prefer to share a part-time desk at work with another telecommuter on a different schedule. Others opt for the short commute to one of the satellite offices some companies have established in more rural communities.

Dialing in to Online Services

Why go online? For starters, online services are a good vehicle for E-mail, which can save time, and sometimes money, over postal mail. In addition, consider these basic business services:

- Business banking
- Daily news
- Book and magazine archives
- Marketing research
- Stock reports
- Business name searches
- Credit searches
- Business forums
- Professional listings
- Airline and hotel reservation systems
- Tax and investment help
- Online catalog shopping
- Real-time exchanges with colleagues

It's easy to see that if you use just a couple of the features you'll save a lot of running-around time. And depending on your field, an online connection can make you more visible while allowing you to plug into up-to-the-minute developments.

Several popular online services are listed on page 127. Many have local access numbers that help keep phone costs down. Some serve as "gateways" to the Internet. Most services have trial offers that let you travel through the system and see what it can do.

Bulletin-board services (BBSs) are more informal than commercial online services. Many are free, and most others are reasonably priced. There may be one in your field; ask around.

Surfing the 'Net

The infamous Internet is not an online service; it's a network of networks, and one of increasingly staggering proportions.

Unlike most formal online services, no one "started" the Internet. It grew out of government and scientific database systems, began to accumulate worldwide sources, and gradually became privatized. Now it's the product of many diverse users, and its wild-and-woolly sprawl reflects that.

The Internet is a great vehicle for long-distance E-mail. In addition, you have access to thousands of user groups on thousands of subjects, huge databases, entire library systems, and far-reaching professional information.

But while the Internet can prove richly rewarding for those who navigate its depths, it's a much bumpier voyage for beginners than with the online services. In most cases, it runs on a string of terse acronyms and computer commands instead of an online service's graphic interface. Just reading about it can give you a headache.

The best Internet introduction for novices is through a gateway on one of the commercial online services. Or ask a knowledgeable friend to guide you. Gophers, Archies, and other local indexes are beginning to bring order to some Internet realms. And menu-driven interfaces are sure to follow.

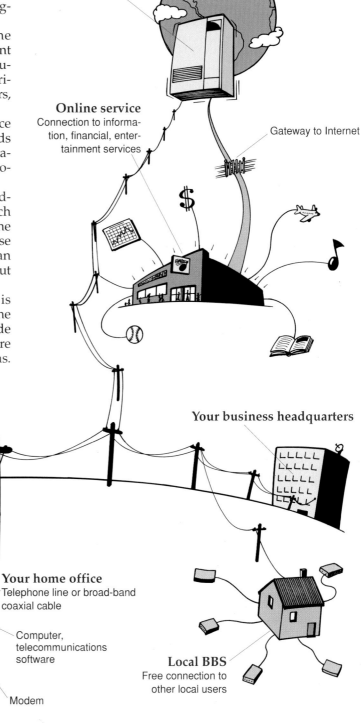

The Internet
Global information network

Online service
Connection to information, financial, entertainment services

Gateway to Internet

Your business headquarters

Your home office
Telephone line or broad-band coaxial cable

Computer, telecommunications software

Modem

Local BBS
Free connection to other local users

units, and some include mailboxes and call forwarding like the big boys. A digital weak point: most allow only 15 minutes' or so worth of messages.

Features to look for include a digital display that alerts you to messages; a time/date stamp; hassle-free remote retrieval; remote activation (in case you forgot to turn on the machine); and voice-controlled operation (called VOX), which lets the caller talk as long as necessary, rather than within a time limit.

Voice-mail options. Many small-business people worry about sounding small, a trait they associate with the lowly answering machine. Others want menu options they can't get from desktop machines. Or they want callers to hear their greeting when they're busy on another line.

Enter the age of voice mail, available in two forms: as a phone-company service or via your personal computer.

Phone-company message centers are an economical option. The service comes in both residential and business versions; the difference is multiple mailboxes and menus, and price. Unfortunately, voice mail is not available in all areas.

Now there are also voice-mail expansion cards available for your computer. Some include call forwarding and even allow callers to play back and edit their own messages. The tinny digital sound bothers some but not all. A few voice-mail programs include other services, too—like automatic faxing when a client requests a price sheet.

MODEMS

A revolutionary tool for many home businesses, the modem opens computer access to the outside world. Through a telephone line, you can send and access information between your home computer and another computer, any distance away.

Your first choice is between internal or external. It's a question of space, and whether or not you'll also be buying a fax (see below). Some prefer to monitor an external modem in use; others like it out of sight. You can also still find portable modems, handy for some road warriors.

Speed is almost everything. Standard baud rates (the unit of measurement) range from 2,400 up to 28,800; a 14,400-baud modem, now standard, costs little more than slower versions. The modem you choose should be Hayes-compatible. If you're opting for an internal model, most experts recommend a fax modem combination; it costs very little more.

FAX MACHINES

The now-familiar fax machine transmits documents via phone lines to another fax or to a computer—almost instantly.

Again, the first question is internal or external? An internal fax modem saves paper and lets you send documents directly from the computer, usually faster and with better resolution than a separate, external fax.

But some people don't want to leave their computers on simply to

A PHONE SERVICE SAMPLER

Many phone companies are making new efforts to meet home-office needs. You'll find residential lines; business lines; custom 800 numbers for small businesses; and numerous rate packages. It's best to contact the phone company directly about their services and what each means.

Here's a checklist of add-on features you may wish to consider.

■ Call waiting. The controversial signal that indicates you have another call while on the line. Some love it; many callers hate it.

■ Busy call forwarding. Redirects calls when you're on the line (for example, to a second line hooked to an anwering machine or voice-mail service). Allows one to spare clients and friends from call waiting.

■ Delayed call forwarding. Routs calls to a designated number after several rings. (You have the option to pick up.)

■ Three-way calling. Allows you to hold triangulated phone "conferences."

■ Priority call forwarding. Sends calls from selected numbers to another location or to your cellular phone, which can keep cellular costs down.

■ Caller ID. Gives you the number of the last caller (illegal in some states).

■ Distinctive ringing. Priority numbers you select have an identifiable ring.

receive faxes, or wish to send documents that aren't computer-based. So some home workers now have both internal and external versions.

In external machines, plain paper is the way to go. Though you'll spend more, prices are falling, and you won't need to recopy slimy thermal-print faxes to preserve them.

To ensure compatibility, look for a Group 3 machine, today's standard. A paper cutter avoids having long rolls of fax paper scrolling across your office floor; a document feeder frees you from standing over the machine and force-feeding one sheet at a time. Built-in memory lets you bypass busy signals, store material for a later time when phone rates are lower, or hold an incoming fax in memory if you've run out of paper. Some faxes have a half-tone setting; look for these if you work with photos or graphics.

DESKTOP COPIERS

If you own a fax, you can use it for emergency copies, but even a plain-paper model is limited to the things that can be scrolled through it. That's where a compact desktop copier comes in handy.

Features to consider include quick warm-up time or standby mode, copying speed, the capacity for both single-sheet and automatic paper feed, reduction/enlargement capability, and the ability to take different sizes of paper (letter and legal sizes, for example). And what about color? The more of these features you need, the bigger the copier will be—and the more it will cost. Also factor in the price of replacement cartridges.

Would you prefer a movable platen or one that stays put? Both types produce good copies, but moving platens require extra space and can be awkward when copying books or other bulky objects.

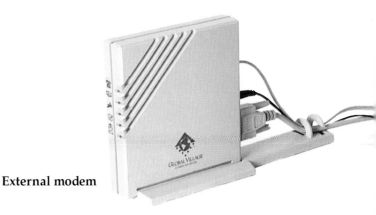

External modem

Plain-paper fax

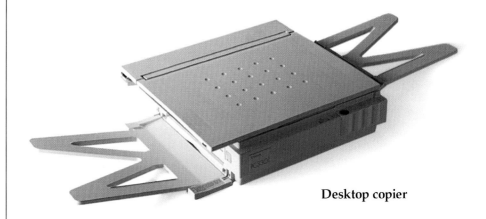

Desktop copier

INFORMATION SOURCES

Whether you're shopping for office electronics or working with a designer or cabinetmaker to create custom storage solutions, you'll find a wealth of ideas and information in brochures offered by the manufacturers and associations listed here. They can also direct you to local outlets and distributors. The addresses and phone numbers in this list are accurate as of press time.

Out in the country or too busy to shop? We've included numerous mail-order sources—some carrying electronics, some furnishings, and others office supplies. And if you're itching to network, you'll find the names and numbers of major online services.

We've concentrated on the products shown in our photos—and, as space allowed, have included other widely available national brands. The yellow pages of your telephone directory can help you locate office suppliers, computer stores, home centers, designers, architects, and other manufacturers and associations near you.

AGENCIES & ASSOCIATIONS

American Home Business Association
(offers various discounts & Internet access)
4505 S. Wasatch Boulevard
Salt Lake City, UT 84124
801-273-5450

Internal Revenue Service
publications & tax forms:
800-TAX-FORM
recorded tapes:
800-829-4477, ext. 123

National Association of Home Based Businesses
(works with entrepreneurs and their specific business needs)
P.O. Box 30220
Baltimore, MD 21270
410-363-3698

Occupational Safety and Health Administration (OSHA)
Publications Office
200 Constitution Avenue NW
Room N-3101
Washington, DC 20210
202-523-9667

Service Corps of Retired Executives (SCORE)
(part of SBA, offers free one-on-one counseling)
409 3rd Street SW
Washington, DC 20024
800-634-0245

Small Business Administration (SBA)
(prerecorded tapes, publications, electronic bulletin board & free small business starter kit)
409 3rd Street SW
Washington, DC 20024
800-827-5722

MAIL-ORDER: COMPUTERS & PERIPHERALS

Action Computer Supplies
P.O. Box 5004
Fremont, CA 94537
800-822-3132

Austin Direct (PC)
2121 Energy Drive
Austin, TX 78758
800-483-9938

CDW Computer Centers, Inc.
1020 E. Lake Cook Road
Buffalo Grove, IL 60089
800-326-4239

Mac Mall
2645 Maricopa Street
Torrance, CA 90503
800-222-2808

MacWarehouse
P.O. Box 3013
Lakewood, NJ 08701
800-255-6227

MicroWarehouse (PC)
P.O. Box 3013
Lakewood, NJ 08701
800-367-7080

PC and MacConnection
14 Mill Street
Marlow, NH 03456
800-800-2222

PCs Compleat
34 St. Martin Drive
Marlborough, MA 01752
800-775-4727

The Mac Zone
15815 S.E. 37th Street
Bellevue, WA 98006
800-436-0606

The PC Zone
15815 S.E. 37th Street
Bellevue, WA 98006
800-258-8088

MAIL-ORDER: FURNITURE & ACCESSORIES

Hello Direct
(telecommunications products)
5884 Eden Park Place
San Jose, CA 95138
800-444-3556

Hold Everything
P.O. Box 7068
San Francisco, CA 94120
800-421-2264

Ikea U.S., Inc.
Plymouth Commons
Plymouth Meeting, PA 19462
610-834-0180

Inmac
2465 Augustine Drive
Santa Clara, CA 95054
800-547-5444

Reliable Home Office
P.O. Box 1502
Ottawa, IL 61350
800-869-6000

The Woodworker's Store
(grommets and wire-management aids)
21801 Industrial Boulevard
Rogers, MN 55374
800-279-4441

MAIL-ORDER: OFFICE SUPPLIES

Paper Access, Inc.
23 W. 18th Street
New York, NY 10011
800-727-3701

Paper Direct
205 Chubb Avenue
Lyndhurst, NJ 07071
800-272-7377

Penny Wise Office Products
4350 Kenilworth Avenue
Edmonston, MD 20781
800-942-3311

Quill
P.O. Box 9408
Palatine, IL 60094
800-789-1331

Viking Office Products
P.O. Box 61144
Los Angeles, CA 90061
800-421-1222

COMPUTER MANUFACTURERS

Apple Computer
Customer Assistance Center
1 Infinity Loop N/S 72P
Cupertino, CA 95014
800-538-9696

Compaq Computer Corporation
Customer Support Center
(PC)
P.O. Box 692000
Houston, TX 77269
800-345-1518

Dell Computer Corporation
(PC)
(catalog sales only)
P.O. Box 203878
Austin, TX 78720
800-289-3355

Digital Equipment Corp.
(PC)
Digital Drive MK01/J25
Merrimack, NH 03054
800-344-4825

Epson Connection Line
P.O. Box 2842
Torrance, CA 90503
800-922-8911

Gateway 2000 (PC)
(catalog sales only)
P.O. Box 2000
North Sioux City, SD 57049
800-846-2000

Hewlett-Packard Company
Customer Information Center
P.O. Box 10301
Palo Alto, CA 94304
800-752-0900

IBM
Old Orchard Road
Armonk, NY 10504
800-772-2227

NEC Technologies
Customer Service and
Support
1414 Massachusetts Avenue
Boxborough, MA 01719
800-388-8888

Packard-Bell
31717 La Tienda Drive
West Lake Village, CA 91362
800-733-5858

Sony Corporation of America
Customer Information Center
1 Sony Drive #56
Parkridge, NJ 07656
800-222-7669

Tektronix, Inc.
P.O. Box 1000
Wilsonville, OR 97070
800-835-9433

Texas Instruments, Inc.
P.O. Box 202230
Austin, TX 78720
800-847-2787

Toshiba America, Inc.
9740 Irvine Boulevard
Irvine, CA 92718
800-468-6744

Visioneer
2860 W. Bayshore Road
Palo Alto, CA 94303
800-787-7007

COMMUNICATIONS

Air Touch Paging
(PacTel, nationwide service)
2181 W. Winton Avenue
Hayward, CA 94545
800-677-6816

AT&T
Small Office Home Office
Product Catalog
24 N. Maple Avenue
Basking Ridge, NJ 07920
800-344-7646

Brother International Corp.
Vantage Court
200 Cottontail Lane
Somerset, NJ 08875
800-284-4329

Canon U.S.A., Inc.
One Canon Plaza
Lake Success, NY 11042
800-652-2666

Global Village (Mac)
(fax/modem and software)
1144 E. Arques Avenue
Sunnyvale, CA 94086
800-736-4821

Hayes Microcomputer Products, Inc.
(modems & communications
software)
P.O. Box 105203
Atlanta, GA 30348
404-441-1617

Motorola Cellular Information Center
600 N. U.S. Highway 45
Libertyville, IL 60048
800-331-6456

Okidata
Customer Information Center
532 Fellowship Road
Mount Laurel, NJ 08054
800-654-3282

Panasonic Communications and Systems
Two Panasonic Way
Mail Stop 7D-3
Secaucus, NJ 07094
800-742-8086

Sharp Electronics Corp.
Sharp Plaza
Mahwah, NJ 07430
800-237-4277

Uniden America Corporation
(cellular phones & pagers)
8707 North by Northeast
Boulevard
Indianapolis, IN 46250
800-364-1944

Xerox Corporation
P.O. Box 1600
Stamford, CT 06904
800-832-6979

OFFICE FURNITURE MANUFACTURERS

Eurodesign, Ltd.
359 State Street
Los Altos, CA 94022
415-941-7761

Herman Miller for the Home
TD Collection
855 E. Main Avenue
P.O. Box 302
Zeeland, MI 49464
800-646-4400

Meridian, Inc.
(a subsidiary of Herman
Miller, Inc.)
18558 171st Avenue
Spring Lake, MI 49456
616-846-0280

Navigator Systems
(work-space systems)
4210 Holden Street
Emeryville, CA 94608
800-653-6280

Sitag
170 W. Technology Drive
Irvine, CA 92718
800-348-0055

Steelcase, Inc.
P.O. Box 1967
Grand Rapids, MI 49501
800-227-2960

Techline by Marshall Erdman and Associates, Inc.
500 S. Division Street
Waunakee, WI 53597
800-356-8400

The Hon Company
P.O. Box 769
Muscatine, IA 52761
800-553-8230

ONLINE SERVICES

America Online, Inc.
8619 Westwood Center Drive
Vienna, VA 22182
800-827-6364

CompuServe
5000 Arlington Center
Boulevard
P.O. Box 20212
Columbus, OH 43220
800-848-8199

Delphi
1030 Massachusetts Avenue
Cambridge, MA 02138
800-695-4005

Genie
401 N. Washington Street
Rockville, MD 20850
800-638-9639

MCI Mail (PC)
(global E-mail)
1801 Pennsylvania Avenue
NW
Washington, DC 20006
800-444-6245

Prodigy Services Co.
445 Hamilton Avenue
White Plains, NY 10601
914-448-2496

TELECOMMUTING

AT&T Telecommuting Connection
(offers a kit that includes a
videotape & handbook)
24 N. Maple Avenue
Basking Ridge, NJ 07920
800-344-2133

networkMCI (PC)
(includes e-mail, fax, document sharing & more)
1801 Pennsylvania Avenue
NW
Washington, DC 20006
800-955-6505

Pacific Bell
(serves California, free
Telecommuting Resource
Guide)
800-378-1980

INDEX

Boldface numbers refer to photographs

Photographers:

Scott Atkinson: 105 bottom right, 112 left; Richard Barnes: 95 bottom left; Dick Busher: 62 bottom; Peter Christiansen: 87; Ben Davidson: 81 bottom; Herb Franklin: 77 bottom; Alan Geller: 52 top; Philip Harvey: 1, 2, 4, 5, 6, 8, 15, 23, 28, 29 top, 30, 32, 33, 34, 35, 36, 37, 38, 39, 40, 41, 42, 43, 44. 45, 46, 47, 48, 49, 50, 51, 52 bottom, 53, 54, 55, 56, 57, 58, 61, 62 top, 63, 64, 65, 66, 67, 68, 69 top left and right, 70, 71, 72, 73, 74, 75, 76, 77 top, 78 bottom, 79, 82 bottom, 83, 84, 85, 88 bottom, 89, 92, 93 bottom right, 94, 95 top and bottom right, 96, 97, 98, 99, 100, 101, 102, 103 top and middle, 104, 105 top left and right, 106, 107, 108, 110, 111, 112 right, 113, 114, 115, 117, 118, 119, 120, 121, 125; Michael Jensen: 7; Elliott Kaufman: 93 top; Norman A. Plate: 78 top, 80 bottom left and right, 81 top, 86, 88 top; Grant Ramaley: 82 top; Kelley Scooter: 93 bottom left; Tim Street-Porter: 29 bottom, 60, 69 bottom, 90; Darrow M. Watt: 80 top left and right; Tom Wyatt: 103 bottom.